BOULANGERIE!

Boulangerie!

POCKET GUIDE TO
PARIS'S FAMOUS BAKERIES

Jack Armstrong
Delores Wilson

Ten Speed Press
Berkeley, California

Ten Speed Press
P.O. Box 7123
Berkeley, California 94707
www.tenspeed.com

Distributed in Australia by Simon and Schuster Australia, in Canada by Ten Speed Press Canada, in New Zealand by Southern Publishing Group, in South Africa by Real Books, in Southeast Asia by Berkeley Books, and in the United Kingdom and Europe by Airlift Books.

Cover design by Toni Tajima
Interior design by Tasha Hall
Illustrations by Monica Dengo

Library of Congress Cataloging-in-Publication Data
   Armstrong, Jack.
      Boulangerie! : pocket guide to Paris's famous bakeries / Jack
   Armstrong, Delores Wilson.
         p.   cm.
      Includes bibliographical references and index.
      ISBN 1-58008-065-0
      1. Baking 2. Cookery, French. 3. Bakers and bakeries—
   France—Paris Guidebooks. I. Wilson, Delores.
   II. Title.
   TX763.A75   1999
   380.1'45641815—dc21   99-14772
                                                        CIP

First printing, 1999
Printed in Canada

1 2 3 4 5 6 7 8 9 10 — 03 02 01 00 99

CONTENTS

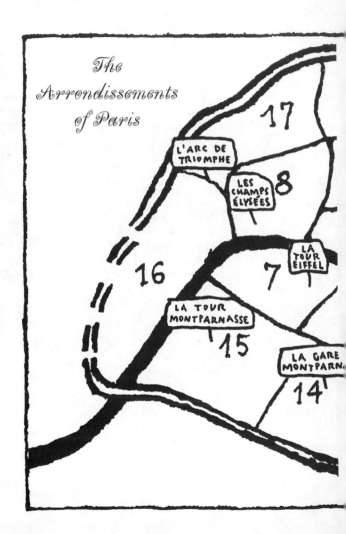

The Arrondissements of Paris

17

L'ARC DE TRIOMPHE

LES CHAMPS ÉLYSÉES

8

LA TOUR EIFFEL

16

7

LA TOUR MONTPARNASSE

15

LA GARE MONTPARN.

14

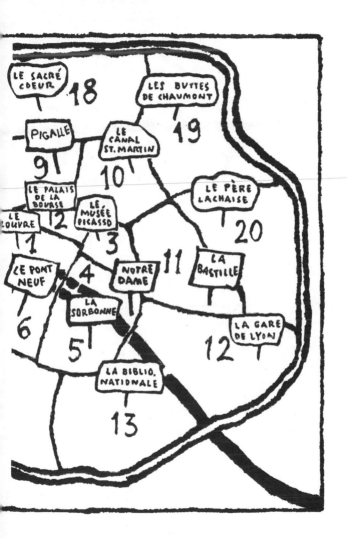

ACKNOWLEDGMENTS

Our special thanks to our two primary translators—Jean-Jacques Vanroyen, Paris, France, and Josiane Réveillé Powell, Plattsburg, Missouri—and to Mary Morgan Vanroyen, Paris, France, who assisted with the research. Their expertise proved invaluable in the completion of this work.

Our sincere appreciation to Bernard Clayton Jr., Bloomington, Indiana, for his helpful advice and encouragement as we pursued this project; to our editors, Lorena Jones and Holly A. Taines, for their direction and patience; to Monica Dengo for the illustrations; to Don Martin and his colleagues at Johnson County Library Merriam, Kansas, for their support and assistance with research; and to Robert Wilson, Shawnee, Kansas, and Alex and Geri Wilson, Lake Minnetonka, Minnesota, for technical advice.

INTRODUCTION

"*Boulangerie*"—you see the signs on the bake shops as you pass on the bus from Orly or Aéroport Charles de Gaulle, or as you disembark the Eurostar at Gare du Nord. Centuries before the Concorde or Michelin tires, before the Bastille or the Louvre, there were boulangeries in France, even in ancient Gaul. *Boule*—round like a ball—is the root of *boulangerie*, referring to the round sourdough loaf, as distinguished from the popular baguette now mass-produced for North American supermarkets. A boulangerie will have both types of bread and much more, with shops often doubling as pâtisseries, baking pastries.

There's Colombian coffee, Swedish meatballs, Belgian waffles, and then there's French cuisine, indisputable pinnacle of the culinary arts. Bread complements every meal on the French table, and the skill of the baker who baked the bread is equal to that of the chef in the kitchen. Bread, and the boulangerie, is vital to life in France.

As a visitor to Paris you face an overwhelming menu of museums, galleries, theaters, monuments, restaurants, and shops. This little book has a single purpose—to help you find and enjoy Paris's tempting, fascinating bakeries. Exploring boulangeries provides the tourist with an intimate look at Paris, an option that is inexpensive, free of long lines, and often only a few yards from a Métro stop.

Some of the boulangers' recipes have been passed on for many generations. As you seek out your favorite boulangerie, you will be exploring the history and legends of Paris. Sample the specialties: baguette, boule, croissant, brioche. Taste life in Paris. Buy some Camembert at a nearby shop, and if you like, a bottle of wine. You're sure to find a bench in the shade in a small park nearby. This is the genuine Paris. Enjoy!

HOW THIS GUIDEBOOK WORKS

In Boulangerie!, you will find 223 selected bakeries listed, representing every arrondissement (district) of Paris. While many other shops were researched, the included boulangeries were chosen for the quality and diversity of their products, their locations, and the attractiveness of their shops. A primary consideration was the response to the question "Faites-vous le pain vous même?" ("Is your bread baked here in your shop?") We listed no bakery unless the answer was "Oui." As of January 1, 1997, the government of France, through its Small Business Ministry, stipulates that only bakeries that select their own flour, knead their own dough, and bake the loaves on the premises may be called boulangeries. This action, the first since prices were decontrolled in 1988, was taken to protect the artisan bakers and the centuries-old traditions of their craft, which have been threatened by mass-produced bread. The bakeries listed in this directory qualify as authentic boulangeries. In many of the boulangeries, we saw wood-fired ovens, often in the basement, and often hundreds of years old and still baking the finest breads in the world.

As you explore, here is the way to locate the bakeries you select. Paris is divided into twenty well-defined arrondissements, each with its own history, culture, and attractions. To really see Paris, one must venture beyond the frequently visited tourist areas into the many and diverse neighborhoods. Our bakeries are listed by arrondissement—one through twenty, some with more bakeries than others—and we give the best means of reaching the bakeries by subway or, in some cases, by bus. We have also listed telephone numbers, as given to us by the boulanger, and the days and hours of operation. Some businesses close in July or August, often for the entire month, so it is wise to call if you are in Paris in late summer, to be assured the bakery is open.

Probably the best way to travel on your search is by the Métro, the Paris subway system. The Métro may be the best subway in the world, with lines reaching to every corner of the city. The subways are clean, remarkably efficient, safe, and inexpensive, with the bonus of delightful art and music at many stations and sometimes even on the train. Métro maps, color coded with line numbers, are free and readily available at ticket booths. You will quickly learn that the Métro lines indicate the destination rather than the direction, so as you plan your bakery exploration, note the end of the line on the Métro route you select. This directory indicates the closest Métro station for each bakery. (These designations were made by the bakery staff at each bakery we interviewed.) When you reach the street, simply say, "Boulangerie," and a friendly person will direct you. Or you might see someone carrying a baguette, a sure sign there is a bakery nearby. As you visit with the boulanger or the bakery staff, ask them to sign your copy of *Boulangerie!* or apply their cachet (rubber stamp) by their shop's listing in the directory. This will please them, and you will have a record of your visit. Street numbers in Paris can be confusing, but we learned that the lower the number on the street the closer it is to the Seine. Many bakeries also list the best autobus (bus) route to reach their shop, so you have this option. The autobus and the Métro accept the same ticket or pass.

We have avoided rating the selected bakeries, because your individual tastes and interests may be different from ours. It is your rating and enjoyment that count.

Voilà!

Jack Armstrong
Delores Wilson

ARRONDISSEMENT

"*The* First," the oldest part of Paris, is said to have more attractions and interesting sights than any other area of like size in the world. It hugs the Seine's right bank from the Place de la Concorde to boulevard de Sébastopol, north five or six blocks to "the Fourth," and includes the west tip of the Île de la Cité to the Pont Neuf, the oldest bridge in Paris. The Jardin des Tuileries and the Musée du Louvre occupy most of the right bank.

The Louvre, every tourist's destination, often for several days, is a mixture of the ancient and the modern. Construction began in the late twelfth century on the fortress that would be converted to a museum and art gallery in 1793. Its entrance, an ultramodern glass pyramid, was commissioned in 1989 by President Mitterrand and designed by I. Ming Pei. At the same time Mitterrand approved the Pei project, he set aside funds for the excavation of the Louvre's courtyard. Visitors can now descend from the pyramid to the twelfth-century dungeons uncovered in the dig. The volume of art treasures in the Louvre and these excavated ruins of Roman walls can be truly overwhelming. The Palais Royal, the Place Vendôme, and the Conciergerie on the Île de la Cité are other attractions of note.

In the early seventies, Les Halles, a subterranean shopping mall located in the northeast quarter of the arrondissement, replaced the city's oldest and most famous market. Its contemporary structure and function offer a stark contrast to the historical preservation for which "the First" is well known. From the park above Les

Halles, however, one can see the beautiful and venerable Église Ste. Eustache, dating from 1532. Completed in 1637, it is the largest Renaissance church in France and is renowned for its music, choir, and concerts.

ℬOULANGERIE ℘ÂTISSERIE 𝒮AINT-ROCH

302, rue Saint Honoré

Métro line 1, Tuileries Station, or Métro line 7 or 14,
  Pyramides Station

Telephone: 01-42-60-58-61

Open daily, except Tuesday, from 7:00 A.M. to 8:00 P.M.

Two short blocks north of the **Jardin des Tuileries** and not much farther from the main entrance to the **Musée du Louvre** is a jewel of a bakery bearing the name of the historic church next door, the **Église Saint-Roch**. M. Soury, maître boulanger, displays the sign of the authentic baker and takes great pride in his breads. Here you will find an impressive display of all the traditional breads, with the bonus of several unique products, including **pain polka,** a bread with a diamond-shaped crust, and a hearty round **pain bûcheron.** He also offers a delightful **puits d'amour** (a jam-filled puff pastry), **mille-feuille** (a layered puff pastry filled with sweetened whipped cream), and his **Opéra Banbourg Saint-Roch.**

Aux Castelblangeois

168, rue Saint Honoré

Métro line 1 or 7, Palais Royal Musée du Louvre Station

Telephone: 01-42-60-77-40

Open daily, except Sunday, from 7:00 A.M. to 8:00 P.M.

On the picturesque rue Saint Honoré we found this small, delightful bakery and salon de thé (tearoom). This bakery has no shortage of quality bread, but what caught our attention was the selection of quiches and tarts. They have **tartelettes aux oignons** (onion tarts), **tartelettes aux épinards** (spinach tarts), **tartelettes au saumon** (salmon tarts), **tartelettes aux champignons** (mushroom tarts), and sandwiches that are neatly packed in plastic and ready to go. They feature a unique pastry, **le pavé du castel.** This shop is a convenient stop for lunch as you visit the **Louvre** and the surrounding area.

Aux Délices de Manon

400, rue Saint Honoré

Métro line 8, 12, or 14, Madeleine Station, or Métro line 1, 8, or
  12, Concorde Station

Telephone: 01-42-60-83-03

Open daily, except Sunday, from 6:30 A.M. to 9:00 P.M.

M. Guy Crouin, maître boulanger, presides over this sparkling clean bake shop and tearoom on the western edge of "the First," close to the **Place de la Concorde** and the **Place Vendôme.** The shop features traditional breads of every size and shape. The chocolates are also impressive. If you wish, you can enjoy the many delicacies available here at the tables inside. The favorite dessert featured here is a delicious biscuit without flour, **entremets le favori.**

𝒟ULOUBE, 𝒥EAN-LOUIS

10, rue du Marché St. Honoré

Métro line 1, Tuileries Station

Autobus route 21, 27, 29, 68, 81, or 95

Telephone: 01-42-61-02-49

Open daily, except Monday, from 6:45 A.M. to 8:00 P.M.

This large boulangerie is located one block north of the **Jardin des Tuileries,** a tempting spot to enjoy the bakery's featured breads and pastries. Their **fougasse,** smothered in black olives and herbs, is especially interesting and tasty.

𝒢OSSELIN, 𝒫HILLIPPE

123–125, rue Saint Honoré

Métro line 1, Louvre Rivoli Station

Autobus route 76

Telephone: 01-45-08-03-59

Open daily, except Monday, from 7:00 A.M. to 8:00 P.M.

Just one block north of the **Louvre,** we discovered this large and friendly bakery with a display of delicacies to stop the most insatiable gourmet: **baguettes anciennes** (old-fashioned baguettes), **brioche, kugelhopf** (a sweet cake with almonds), tarts of all descriptions, **flan, cheese-cake,** and panini sandwiches. It's all there.

JULIEN, JEAN-NOËL
75, rue Saint Honoré
Métro line 1 or 4, Les Halles Station
Telephone: 01-42-36-24-83
Open daily, except Sunday, from 6:30 A.M. to 8:00 P.M.

From the Métro station, you walk through the park area of the **Forum des Halles** to this friendly, very busy neighborhood bakery. M. Julien is proud of the first-place honors awarded his **baguette de tradition** (traditional baguette) in a citywide competition in 1995—and understandably so. Don't miss trying this. He also has many tempting takeouts for lunch or snacks in the nearby park. His prepared salads, ready to go on plastic plates, crêpes, quiches, tarts, croissants, and even pizza caught our eye.

𝓛EBOURG, 𝓖ILLES

45, rue de l'Arbre Sec

Métro line 1, Louvre Rivoli Station, or Métro line 7, Pont Neuf
  Station

Autobus route 7, Pont Neuf or Samaritaine

Telephone: 01-42-60-11-97

Open daily, except Saturday and Sunday, from 7:00 A.M. to 8:00 P.M.

This charming bakery is less than one block from the
Pont Neuf, Paris's oldest bridge, in one direction and
from the busy rue de Rivoli in the other direction. The
Louvre, the **Châtelet,** and **Les Halles** are just a short
walk away. The sign in the window of the bakery says,
"Comme autrefois la vraie baguette française dans votre
ville," indicating that their baguettes are made as they
were in the French past, truly like an old-time loaf. Their
tempting selection of sandwiches, salads, pizza, and
quiches suggests an ideal stop for lunch or a snack when
visiting the Louvre. M. Lebourg takes special pride in his
pain feuilleté au seigle et aux raisins, a raisin rye bread
with puff pastry; a special **rétrodor baguette,** a rustic,
old-fashioned baguette; and **gâteau basque** (Basque
cake).

MAISON CLÉRET

11, rue Jean Lantier

Métro line 1, 4, 7, 11, or 14, Châtelet Station

Telephone: 01-42-33-82-68

Open daily, except Sunday and Monday, from 7:00 A.M. to 8:00 P.M.

On the corner of rue Jean Lantier and rue des Lavandières Saint-Opportune, close to the **Place du Châtelet** and only a short distance over the **Pont au Change** from **Notre-Dame,** we were fortunate to discover this jewel of a bakery. Neatly appointed with tile, wood, and glass, they display breads of all kinds in round baskets, in tall baskets, and in large, flat baskets. Special breads of note include **pain à l'ancienne,** an old-fashioned loaf with a touch of fermentation, and **pain de seigle aux noix** (rye bread with nuts). They also bake assorted **fougasses,** with gruyère, onions, olives, and more, and elegant chocolate cakes in abundance. There is a lovely small room with tables and chairs, with an entrance from the bakery, where you can enjoy your purchases, or you may choose to sit at one of the small round tables outside the bakery, where there is a crib with old or rejected bread, yours for the taking.

ℳAX ℘OILÂNE

42, Place du Marché St. Honoré

Métro line 7 or 14, Pyramides Station

Autobus route 68

Telephone: 01-42-61-10-53

Open daily, except Saturday and Sunday, from 9:00 A.M. to 6:30 P.M.

The name Poilâne is so well known that it is almost synonymous with Paris's boulangeries. Two brothers, Lionel and Max, operate separately, both following in the footsteps of their equally well known father, Premier Boulanger Pierre Poilâne. One of three bakeries operated by Max Poilâne is one block from the avenue de l'Opéra, and there you will find a treasure of products, including the famed country loaf of immense proportions—sold whole, by the piece, or by the slice. The **petits pains aux raisins et aux noix** (small dinner rolls with raisins or nuts), **tartelettes aux pommes** (apple tarts), and his **feuilleté au jambon et au fromage** (ham and cheese in a flaky pastry) are all irresistible.

His other two locations are at 87, rue Brancion, in "the Fifteenth," and 29, rue de l'Ouest, in "the Fourteenth."

𝒫LAISIRS & 𝒫AINS

215, rue Saint Honoré

Métro line 1, Louvre Rivoli Station

Telephone: 01-42-61-18-04

Open daily, except Sunday, from 7:00 A.M. to 7:00 P.M.

With the **Louvre** a short walk away, this is another bakery with tempting snacks before or after your visit to the world's most famous museum. Their crêpe machine can be pushed onto the sidewalk to accommodate "crêpe only" customers. We liked their **feuilleté au jambon et aux épinards** (puff pastries with ham and spinach) and the **aumônière** ("beggar's purse," a thin, filled crêpe wrapped like a bundle). At least ten different breads are listed on the placard in the shop. We observed a delivery truck taking large sacks of baguettes, probably headed for a restaurant or elsewhere for resale.

ARRONDISSEMENT

"The Second" has its own character and distinction, with the Galerie Colbert and the Galerie Vivienne, remaining examples of pedestrian streets inside city blocks, in the southwest quarter and le Quartier Juif, the Jewish quarter. In "the Second" you'll also find the Palais de la Bourse, the Paris stock exchange, the financial center of France, with banks and related offices close by. A block or so away from la Bourse is the former home of the Bibliothèque Nationale, the French national library, which competes with the British library as the largest library in western Europe. Since 1642, French law has required that every book published in France be archived in the Bibliothèque Nationale. The vast collection of over twelve million volumes includes two Gutenberg Bibles and the private libraries of all the French monarchs. The library has now outgrown its building on rue de Riche-lieu and has been moved to the thirteenth arrondisse-ment. The eastern edge of "the Second" is the rue St.-Denis, one of the oldest and best-known streets in Paris. This section of the city may have fewer bakeries than most arrondissements, but we discovered several very good ones.

NARD

53, rue Montorgueil

Métro line 4, Les Halles Station

Telephone: 01-42-33-31-05

Open daily from 6:30 A.M. to 9:00 P.M.

This bakery has thirty varieties of bread, but there is more. You will find the familiar, crusty, pretzel-like **fougasse** in smaller sizes, with endless varieties of garnishes: onions, anchovies, poppy seeds, olives, bacon, and a variety of cheeses. For a takeout lunch or snack there is stuffed cabbage, cooked pork or ham, and **terrine de saumon** (salmon pâté). Next door is the world-famous **Pâtisserie Stohrer**, founded in 1730, with not only a delightful and charming interior but marvelous pastries—another good reason to discover the white brick street, the rue Montorgueil.

LE LIDEC

16, rue des Petits-Carreaux

Métro line 3, Sentier Station

Telephone: 01-42-36-54-29

Open daily, except Sunday and Monday, from 6:30 A.M. to 8:00 P.M.

M. le Lidec operates this small, very attractive bakery with a great selection of breads. **Pain paillasse,** an artisanal loaf, is especially appealing. The pastry shelves include **sablés** (shortbread biscuits), **tuiles aux amandes** (almond-flavored cookies), **éclairs,** and an interesting pastry to be eaten "only on Saturdays," **ralettes.** They list the Jewish Quarter, le Quartier Juif, as an interesting section of the area.

MESNIL LA FORNARINA

90, rue Montorgueil

Métro line 3, Sentier Station

Autobus route 79

Telephone: 01-42-33-09-13

Open daily, except Monday and Tuesday, from 6:30 A.M. to 8:30 P.M.

Monsieur and Madame Mesnil evidence great pride in their sparkling clean bakery on the picturesque rue Montorgueil. They feature **pain aux six céréales et aux trois graines** (bread with six different grains and three types of seeds), **brioche suisse, boules de campagne,** and **sablé au** chocolat et aux noix (shortbread with chocolates and nuts). They also sell **flan,** pizza, sandwiches, and more for takeout.

Au Panetier (B. Lebon)

10, Place des Petits-Pères

Métro line 3, Bourse Station

Autobus route 29 to Notre-Dame des Victoires

Telephone: 01-42-60-90-23

Open daily, except Saturday and Sunday, from 8:00 A.M. to 7:15 P.M.

Founded in 1902, facing **Notre-Dame des Victoires** and a short walk from Paris's stock exchange, is this excellent bakery, with a distinctive green front. Inside it is decorated with beautiful and unusual tiles behind the bread displays. M. Lebon offers a seemingly endless variety of breads and pastries baked in his old wood-fired oven, featuring large and small loaves of **pain de campagne au pavot** (country-style bread with poppy seeds) and **pain de seigle aux noix** (rye bread with nuts). They also offer pastries, a large selection of small, thin cookies, and chocolate bars and mints.

$\mathcal{R}$OLIN

149, rue Montmartre

Métro line 3, Bourse Station

Autobus route 48 or 87

Telephone: 01-42-32-14-69

Open daily, except Saturday and Sunday, from 7:00 A.M. to
8:00 P.M.

In a very nice neighborhood near the **Palais de la Bourse,**
the stock exchange, is a small, busy bakery with many
attractions. You will like their variety of special breads—
petits seigles aux raisins (small loaves of raisin rye),
campagne au son et seigle complet (a country-style bran
and rye whole-grain bread), and **viennoises au chocolat**
(Viennese pastries with chocolate). These master bakers
have two other shops in the city: one in the twelfth
arrondissement, at 23, rue de Lyon, and one in "the Thirteenth," at 184, avenue de Choisy.

$\mathcal{L}$ES $\mathcal{T}$ROIS $\mathcal{C}$IGOGNES

4, rue des Petits-Carreaux

Métro line 3, Sentier Station, or Métro line 1, 4, 7, 11, or 14,
Châtelet Station

Telephone: 01-42-33-77-70

Open daily, except Wednesday and Thursday, from 6:30 A.M. to
8:30 P.M.

Les Trois Cigognes is a busy bakery, both inside and on the street, where their sidewalk display case tempts passing pedestrians. We have seen **baguettes circulaires** (round baguettes) before, but here they are in abundance. The proprietors sell **florentines** (nougatine cookies), **pâtes de fruit** (pastries with fruit), chocolates, sandwiches, and much more. The large shopping mall **Forum des Halles** is nearby.

ARRONDISSEMENT

$\mathcal{T}$he third arrondissement, together with part of "the Fourth," is known as the Marais (marsh or swamp). It was a marsh for centuries, but thirteenth-century monks drained it to make it more habitable. By the early seventeenth century, the Marais had become the center of fashionable living, and large hôtels particuliers (mansions) were built, many of them masterpieces of architecture. Some remain as museums and galleries.

The Marais has been the victim of modernization, as some medieval streets were widened and new codes enacted. It has, however, survived and retained much of its historical charm. Les Archives Nationales (the national archives) are housed in the Hôtel Soubise, built in 1705. The Hôtel de Rohan, built about the same time, is among the most famous old mansions. On the rue Vielle du Temple, which runs by the Hôtel de Rohan, there are several other mansions of note. Added attractions in this most interesting section of the city are the Musée Picasso, located in the Hôtel Salé; the Musée de l'Histoire de France; the Musée des Techniques; and the Conservatoire National des Arts et Métiers.

La Fougasse

25, rue de Bretagne

Métro line 8, Filles du Calvaire Station, or Métro line 3, 8, 9, or 11,
República Station

Telephone: 01-42-72-36-80

Open daily, except Monday, from 7:00 A.M. to 2:30 P.M. and
from 4:30 P.M. to 8:15 P.M.

Taking its name from the traditional bread delicacy **la fougasse,** this bakery features several varieties with cheese, olives, herbs, and spices and an abundant variety of other popular breads, in shapes and sizes to please every customer. The pastry assortment features **tropézienne,** a cream-filled delight from Saint Tropéz, and they also sell crêpes and croissants with ham and cheese. A push-out counter makes it easy for takeouts to nearby parks. They make their own chocolate too.

V. GARCIA

138, rue Vielle du Temple

Métro line 8, St. Sébastien Froissart Station

Telephone: 01-42-71-30-36

Open daily, except Sunday, from 7:30 A.M. to 8:30 P.M.

In the Temple Quarter of "the Third," M. Vincent Garcia operates this appealing bakery with a huge inventory of specialties, including **pain de mie,** a small white loaf made for sandwiches; **pain complet** (whole-grain bread); and baguettes of several dimensions. The display of meringues and chocolates, also made in the shop, is irresistible.

J. M. LEPRÊTRE

38, rue de Bretagne

Métro line 3, 8, 9, or 11, République Station

Telephone: 01-42-78-00-86

Open daily, except Monday and Sunday afternoon and evening,
    from 6:45 A.M. to 8:00 P.M.

This large, pleasant corner bakery was very busy on the Saturday morning we visited. M. Leprètre displays the familiar blue authentic baker's sign and produces the line of breads to qualify—boules, baguettes, petit pain, and more. There are many takeout items—sandwiches and pastries—in addition to the wonderful breads and a park, the **Square du Temple,** in which to enjoy them just a short walk away.

Au Levain du Marais

32, rue de Turenne

Métro line 8, Chemin Vert Station

Autobus route 96

Telephone: 01-42-78-07-31

Open daily, except Sunday, from 7:00 A.M. to 8:00 P.M.

On the corner of rue de Turenne and rue du Foin, in the Marais, we discovered this delightful bakery run by the friendly baker M. Thierry Rabineau and his wife, Dominique. Until 1994, M. Rabineau, who recently received high honors for his **baguette,** worked for the Moulin de la Vierge bakery, which he left to open this shop. The bakery has an attractive marblelike exterior with picturesque glass side panels. The wood-paneled interior is likewise charming, with a lovely tile ceiling set off by a handsome chandelier. M. and Mme. Rabineau offer excellent-quality breads, quiches, and pastries. **Pain au levain—campagne, complet et seigle** (country-style, whole-wheat and rye)—and **fougasse,** the ubiquitous twisted dough concoction, are listed as their specialties. They also have three bakeries in Japan.

La Normande

134, rue de Turenne

Métro line 3, 8, 9, or 11, République Station

Telephone: 01-42-78-04-72

Open daily, except Sunday, from 7:00 A.M. to 8:30 P.M.

Here we found a marvelous delicacy filled with chunks of chocolate—**la viennoise aux pépites de chocolat.** While this specialty caught our eye, and our appetite, there is more. We counted fifteen different breads, of every shape and size. They gladly cut the standard baguette in half and charged two, not four, francs, about forty cents in U.S. currency, a common practice among boulangeries.

Onfroy

34, rue de Saintonge

Métro line 8, Filles du Calvaire Station

Autobus route 96 or 20

Telephone: 01-42-77-56-46

Open daily, except Saturday afternoon and Sunday, from 7:45 A.M.
to 1:30 P.M. and from 3:00 P.M. to 8:00 P.M.

M. Fernand Onfroy, from Normandy, opened this bakery at 34, rue de Saintonge, in 1965. The first known bakery on this site was opened in 1628, but the discovery of two ancient ovens at different levels on the property suggests the possibility of bakeries on this site even earlier. M. Onfroy features several special breads, all baked in his wood-fired oven: **pain au fromage et aux noix** (bread with cheese and nuts), **pain aux raisins et aux algues** (bread with raisins and edible seaweed), an especially rich, dark **pain de seigle** (rye bread), a **baguette biologique** (an organic baguette) and a **baguette complète** (whole-wheat baguette). The bakery is not far from the **Musée Picasso** and the **Centre Georges Pompidou**.

$\mathscr{P}$ATEAU, $\mathscr{F}$REDERIC

6, rue du Pas de la Mule

Métro line 8, Chemin Vert Station, or Métro line 1, 5, or 8, Bastille Station

Autobus route 29 or 65 on blvd. Beaumarchais

Telephone: 01-42-78-52-17

Open daily, except Monday, from 7:00 A.M. to 8:30 P.M.

Close by this bakery is a very attractive park, the **Place des Vosges**, and in the neighborhood are several museums of note: **Musées Victor Hugo, Carnavalet,** and **Picasso.**

Inside, the boulangerie has a counter along three walls, with chairs where you can relax with a cold drink or juice, or you can sit at a table while enjoying the **duchesse normande (pomme, crème d'amande, nougatine),** an irresistible apple and almond cream dessert, or their chocolate, pear, or almond tarts. M. Pateau's baguettes are especially noteworthy, featuring one **maxi aux céréales,** a unique loaf, and the familiar long and thin **ficelle.**

ARRONDISSEMENT

*I*f the importance of an attraction in Paris is determined by the number of tour buses, the Cathédrale de Notre-Dame de Paris, on the Île de la Cité in the "Fourth," is a sure winner. This is the oldest part of the city, the site of a Christian church as early as the late sixth century that was destroyed by the Norman invaders, rebuilt, and then razed to make room for Notre-Dame in the twelfth century. The Île de la Cité, connected by a footbridge to the other island in the Seine, the Île St. Louis, does indeed give the arrondissement historical distinction. Just across the river is the Hôtel de Ville, the city hall of Paris, an imposing structure and courtyard dating to the sixteenth century. Much of "the Fourth" was spared the reconstruction of Baron Haussmann, who modernized much of Paris as a minister for Napoléon III, so the attraction of its medieval streets and stately hôtels particuliers (mansions) remains. The Place des Vosges in the northeast quarter is the oldest public square in Paris, and one of the most charming. In stark contrast to the authentic history throughout the arrondissement is the Centre Georges Pompidou, visible all too clearly from most parts of the arrondissement, with its inside-out architecture and outside escalators taking you to the seventh-story rooftop. The Centre's cobblestone courtyard does offer some relief, however, and here street mimes and other performers entertain the tourists. The winding narrow streets of the Marais, the rue des Rosiers, the heart of the Paris Quartier Juif (Jewish quarter), the magnificence of Notre-Dame, the legend of Victor Hugo, and the matchless charm of the Île St. Louis qualify "the Fourth" as the section of the city you are likely to enjoy most.

Aux Délices St. Paul

129, rue St. Antoine
Métro line 1, St. Paul Station
Autobus route 96
Telephone: 01-42-72-32-91
Open daily, except Sunday, from 6:15 A.M. to 8:30 P.M.

Midway between the **Hôtel de Ville** and the **Place de la Bastille,** we discovered this fascinating bakery. The boulanger is quick to tell you that he specializes in **artisanaux** (craft bakery products) and calls your attention to several. We liked the **pain de campagne** (country loaf), the **pain de mie** (white, thin-crusted bread for sandwiches), a delicious **pain de seigle** (rye bread), and a distinctive **pain de son** (bran bread). They also have fancy pastries and takeout sandwiches for your enjoyment.

𝒢UERINEAU

29, rue St. Antoine

Métro line 1, 5, or 8, Bastille Station, or Métro line 1, St. Paul
  Station

Autobus route 69 or 76

Telephone: 01-48-04-09-04

Open daily, except Wednesday, from 7:00 A.M. to 8:00 P.M.

A short walk from the **Place des Vosges,** we visited this very attractive bakery and pastry shop that offers many traditional breads. The cream-filled **mille-feuille** caught our eye, as did their **fougasse,** one with unusual herbs and garnish. We have tried many **financiers,** but Guerineau's almond cakes have something extra. There are also tarts large and small, sweet rolls much like our "danish," flan, and chocolates.

𝒥o 𝒢OLDENBERG

7, rue des Rosiers

Métro line 1, St. Paul Station

Autobus route 96

Telephone: 01-48-87-20-16

Open daily from 8:30 A.M. to 11:00 P.M.

If this directory selected famous delicatessens, Jo Goldenberg, in the **Marais,** would be close to the top of the list. Customers stand in line to buy bagels and Jewish rye bread reminiscent of the New York rye bread once available on 55th Street in Hyde Park, Chicago. Do not expect a full-scale bakery, but it is a highly recommended luncheon stop.

𝓜ARCIAUNO

14–16, rue des Rosiers

Métro line 1, St. Paul Station

Autobus route 96

Telephone: 01-48-87-48-88

Open daily, except Saturday, from 8:00 A.M. to 9:00 P.M.

If you are seeking an authentic Jewish bakery, here is your boulanger. He features traditional breads and pastries from old family recipes. We like the **pain de mie** (sandwich bread), **pain au cumin** (bread with caraway), and **pain de seigle juif** (Jewish rye). They also sell pastries: **croquets aux amandes** (almond croquettes), **strudel aux pommes** (apple strudel), **sablés aux amandes** (almond cookies), and, of course, **cheesecake.**

MARTIN PHILLIPPE

40, rue St. Louis en l'Île

Métro line 7, Pont Marie Station

Autobus route 67 to rue des Deux Ponts

Telephone: 01-43-54-69-48

Open daily, except Sunday and Monday, from 7:00 A.M. to

1:30 P.M. and from 3:30 P.M. to 8:00 P.M.

The **Île St. Louis,** where this boulangerie is located, is a unique, historical jewel in the old Paris. Located across the charming, narrow rue St. Louis en l'Île from the **Église St. Louis** is this equally charming bakery, in business since 1930. They feature baguettes and pastries in the old style: **pain au levain** (leavened bread), a special **pain de seigle "correzien,"** mille-feuille, the pretzel-shaped **fougasse,** and **brioche feuilletée** (a special puff pastry). A great stop!

RACHINEL

87, rue St. Antoine

Métro line 1, 5, or 8, Bastille Station, or Métro line 1, St. Paul

Station

Telephone: 01-48-87-87-59

Open daily, except Monday, from 6:30 A.M. to 8:30 P.M.

Here is a very busy corner bakery with a coffee bar. They have a full line of bread, you should note particularly the **pain de seigle aux raisins** (raisin rye) and a special improved loaf, **pain amelioré.** You will like the **croque-monsieur,** a ham and cheese sandwich topped with more cheese and toasted, and the **croque-madame,** a croque-monsieur with an egg on top. Pastry features include **tartelettes viennoises** (Viennese tarts), extra-large meringues, and **financiers** (small almond cakes). The **Place de la Bastille** is just a short walk down the street.

Rioux, Alain

35, rue des Deux Ponts

Métro line 7, Pont Marie Station

Autobus route 67 to rue des Deux Ponts

Telephone: 01-43-54-57-59

Open daily, except Thursday and Friday, from 6:45 A.M. to 8:15 P.M.

This very small, but complete, bakery on the Île St. Louis displays authentic breads and many pastries. We like their **seigle royal, galette de pain viennois,** a flat bread, and their heavy-crusted **baguette.** M. Rioux recommends his special pastries: the **St. Louis mendiant** (a tart with almonds, figs, raisins, and nuts), a **tarte à la framboise-coco** (raspberry-coconut pie), and **croquets suisses noix-pistaches** (cream cheese on crackers with pistachios). **Le financier,** the frequently seen almond-flavored dessert, is at its best from M. Rioux, who also adds another favorite, **cookise,** a special chocolate cookie. His bakery was near our apartment, and we frequently stopped in for bread and his special pastries.

ARRONDISSEMENT

*T*his arrondissement is best known as the Latin Quarter, and though the early Romans may have built some of the ancient streets, *Latin* refers to the language of the scholars residing near the famous Sorbonne and the University of Paris. The University of Paris was founded in 1170, with earlier roots as the cathedral school of Notre-Dame. Robert de Sorbon founded the Sorbonne as the theological faculty in 1253. The influence of this most famous part of the university is legendary, and through the centuries the Sorbonne has, in effect, been the identity of the university. There have been several reorganizations through the years, most recently in the late sixties and early seventies to its present state as the Universities of Paris I–XIII, designating a sprawling complex of thirteen colleges in several parts of the city, with an enrollment of 160,000 students. The old buildings of the Sorbonne, on the rue des Écoles preserve the historic legacy of the Quartier Latin. The rue Mouffetard, where you find the Mouffetard market, is one of the oldest streets in Paris.

The Sorbonne and the Latin Quarter, the poets and artists, and the philosophers and Philistines of St. Germain des Prés all belong to "the Fifth." The arrondissement is bounded by the Seine on the north, the Jardin des Plantes to the south, the national museum of natural history, and a nature park dating to 1640 with every attraction the nature lover craves—including dinosaur skeletons, rare animals, quartz formations, and tropical plants. Sight-seeing highlights of "the Fifth" include the

Panthéon, whose proud dome is visible from many points in the Latin Quarter; the Église St. Étienne du Mont, with its rose windows; the Arènes de Lutèce (Lutèce is the ancient name for Paris), a Roman amphitheater whose ruins were unearthed during the construction of rue Monge and restored around 1910; and the Musée de Cluny, which houses one of the world's finest collections of medieval art, jewelry, architecture, and tapestry.

BEAUVALLET ET JULIEN

6 rue de Poissy

Métro line 10, Maubert-Mutualité Station

Autobus route 63

Telephone. 01-43-26-94-24

Open daily, except Wednesday, from 7:00 A.M. to 8:00 P.M

The boulanger-patron at this bakery came from Morocco to Paris, where he apprenticed to become a baker. Noted specialties are **pain au levain artisanal fait à la main,** a leavened bread made by this artisan craftsman baker, and an award-winning **baguette.** The location is delightful and within steps of the bridges to **Île de la Cité, Notre-Dame,** and **Île St. Louis.**

ℬOULANGERIE DES 𝒜RÈNES

31, rue Monge

Métro line 10, Cardinal Lemoine Station

Autobus route 27, 47, 97, or 83

Telephone: 01-43-26-29-29

Open daily, except Tuesday and Wednesday, from 7:00 A.M. to
8:30 P.M.

Specialties include bell-shaped **pain aux noix** (bread with walnuts), **pain aux raisins et aux noix** (raisin bread with nuts), **flamme** (oval flame-shaped pizza), crêpes, jams and jellies of every description, and **croissants ordinaires** (traditional croissants).

ℬOULANGERIE 𝒢ARCIA

52, blvd. St. Germain

Métro line 10, Maubert-Mutualité Station

Autobus route 91 or 67

Telephone: 01-43-54-48-72

Open daily, except Sunday, from 7:00 A.M. to 8:00 P.M.

Patron C. Garcia offers a complete assortment of breads and pastries. We were especially attracted to his **pain au levain et aux céréales** (leavened whole-cereal bread) and the dark, sour **baguette à l'ancienne.** You will be most pleased with any bread you select here.

Le Cardinal

68, rue du Cardinal Lemoine

Métro line 10, Cardinal Lemoine Station

Autobus route 47

Telephone: 01 43-26-34-62

Open daily, except Monday, from 7:00 A.M. to 8:00 P.M.

This small, friendly bakery's specialties include **pain à l'ancienne** and **pain au levain,** with some pastries, packaged cookies, and candies. A few doors down the street, at 74, rue du Cardinal Lemoine, is a marker announcing that Ernest Hemingway (1899–1961) lived there from 1922 to 1923.

De l'Entracte

70, blvd. St. Marcel

Métro line 7, Les Gobelins Station

Autobus route 91

Telephone: 01-47-07-22-40

Open daily, except Wednesday, from 7:00 A.M. to 8:30 P.M.

This bakery has an impressive line of **boules, baguettes,** and **brioches,** sandwiches, chocolates, and flan. The ruins of the **Arènes de Lutèce** are a short distance from the shop, where you will find a park area to relax and enjoy your lunch or your snack from l'Entracte.

ᏀÉRARD ᏏEAUFORT

6, rue Linné

Métro line 7 or 10, Jussieu Station

Autobus route 67 or 89

Telephone: 01-47-07-10-94

Open daily, except Saturday and Sunday, from 7:30 A.M. to 8:00 P.M.

There are good reasons to remember M. Beaufort's marvelous bakery: first, the wood-fired oven where we saw the **baguettes,** dozens of them, pulled from the fire, and moments later were allowed to sample one, and second, location. The boulangerie is just a short walk from the **Jardin des Plantes** and even closer to the ancient Roman amphitheater, the **Arènes de Lutèce.** Here you will find the rue des Boulangers, the Street of Bakers, now without a single bake shop. Specialties featured at this boulangerie are **croissants aux amandes** (almond croissants), a tasty **tarte aux pommes de terre** (a quiche-like potato pastry), **ficelle,** chocolates, sandwiches, and more. This delightful bakery is very busy, and we were given a high recommendation for their products by one of the customers waiting in line.

GIBOUIN, JEAN-PIERRE

56, blvd. St. Marcel

Métro line 7, Les Gobelins Station

Autobus route 91 or 67

Telephone: 01-43-31-15-39

Open daily, except Monday, from 6:30 A.M. to 8:00 P.M.

Tempting specialties in addition to breads are their **fars bretons aux pruneaux** (Breton sugar cakes with prunes), panini, pizza, crêpes, quiches, flans, chocolates, and sandwiches. They are especially proud of their **pâtisseries royales,** and we highly recommend them.

GRÉGOIRE BENTIVEGNA
(BOULANGERIE MODERNE)

16, rue des Fosses Saint Jacques

Métro line 7, Place Monge Station, or RFR, Luxembourg Station

Autobus route 21 or 58

Telephone: 01-43-54-12-22

Open daily, except Saturday afternoon and Sunday, from 7:30 A.M.
to 8:00 P.M.

This boulangerie is very close to the **Panthéon,** a neo-classical monument described as one of the most beautiful public buildings in the world. Once the **Église Ste. Geneviève,** it was converted to a mausoleum in 1791. Émile Zola, Victor Hugo, Voltaire, and Rousseau are buried here. Across the plaza from the Panthéon is the

mairie (town hall) for "the Fifth," and here also is this charming bakery, with a glass tile ceiling and a trim of the same tiles around the top of the walls. Specialties include **brioche aux raisins** and **brioche au chocolat,** a unique Basque cornbread, flan, éclairs, croissants, quiches, and an attractive selection of takeouts for the small park across the street.

Jacques Sauvètes

2, rue de Bazeilles

Métro line 7, Censier-Daubenton Station

Autobus route 27 or 47

Telephone: 01-47-07-35-40

Open daily, except Monday, from 7:30 A.M. to 8:00 P.M.

Jacques Sauvètes sells an extensive line of bread featuring **pain au levain complet et seigle** (leavened rye), **pain viennois,** and baguettes of several lengths. M. Sauvètes also has an array of sandwiches with cheese and raw vegetables, quiches, and pizza. There is ample fare here for a picnic in the park.

A. LERCH

4, rue du Cardinal Lemoine

Métro line 10, Maubert-Mutualité Station

Autobus route 63, 27, 24, 86, or 87

Telephone: 01-43-26-15-80

Open daily, except Monday and Tuesday, from 7:00 A.M. to 7:30 P.M.

While M. Lerch is better known for his pastries, his breads are also delicious and of excellent quality. We visited the bakery, Pâtisserie-Biscuiterie Alsacienne, in November, six weeks before Christmas, and enjoyed an elaborate display of specialties for Noël: **pain d'épices décorés** (decorated spice bread), **sablé à la canelle** (cinnamon shortbread), **pain à l'anis** (anise bread), and much more. The **Pont de la Tournelle** to the **Île St. Louis** and the **Left Bank** stalls are just a few steps from this appealing bakery.

LESPERON, CLAUDE

23, rue Jussieu

Métro line 7 or 10, Jussieu Station

Telephone: 01-43-54-39-69

Open daily, except Saturday and Sunday, from 6:30 A.M. to 7:30 P.M.

This interesting shop, in a neighborhood with pocket parks and benches nearby, has a crêpe machine and sandwich display outside, so you can purchase freshly made crêpes and sandwiches to take to a park for lunch or a snack. We were attracted to their wide variety of breads, meringues, and the **tartelettes au citron** (lemon tarts).

Louis Bernard

1, ave. des Gobelins

Métro line 7, Censier-Daubenton Station, or Métro line 10, Cardinal
    Lemoine Station

Telephone: 01-43-31-36-66

Open daily, except Monday, from 6:00 A.M. to 8:00 P.M.

Featured items in this boulangerie are **pain de seigle complet au son, pain de mie viennois,** quiche, candies, sherbet, and an interesting array of takeout sandwiches.

Michel Brusa

16, rue Mouffetard

Métro line 7, Place Monge Station, or Métro line 10, Cardinal
    Lemoine Station

Telephone: 01-47-07-06-36

Open daily, except Sunday, from 7:00 A.M. to 9:00 P.M.

With the pride in his products of an artisan baker, M. Brusa features an old-fashioned sourdough **baguette ancienne** and **pain au levain naturel** (naturally leavened bread). The pastry cases have **tourtes aux épinards** (spinach pies), cakes, meringues, and quiches of all descriptions. This boulangerie is on rue Mouffetard, a busy pedestrian street with fascinating open-air markets, not far from Hemingway's house at 74, rue du Cardinal Lemoine. There is a small park nearby where you can enjoy a snack from M. Brusa's fine shop, and the **Panthéon** is a short walk away.

*M*OUSSAY, *A*NDRÉ

47, ter blvd. St Germain

Métro line 10, Maubert-Mutualité Station

Autobus route 86, 47, 24, or 87

Telephone: 01-43-54-04-14

Open daily from 7:00 A.M. to 8:00 P.M.

Where the rue Monge heads south from boulevard St. Germain, we found a street market in full operation and, as a bonus, this excellent boulangerie. M. André Moussay features a **campagne beauceron aux céréales,** a hearty country-style loaf from a recipe of the Beauce region, and the more common **pain complet** and **pain de seigle.** Sandwiches, quiches, and pizza for takeout are displayed in a large case outside. A short three blocks down the rue Monge you will find the **Arènes de Lutèce,** the remains of a first-century Roman amphitheater, with a beautiful park adjoining. Paris offers no better place for a picnic lunch.

A. Nerrand

28, rue Geoffroy-St. Hilaire

Métro line 7, Censier-Daubenton Station

Autobus route 67 or 89

Telephone: 01-43-31-81-49

Open daily, except Saturday and Sunday, from 7:15 A.M. to 8:15 P.M.

The baker lists his all-cereal bread and his **baguette à l'ancienne** as his specialties. Both are superb and well worth trying. At Christmas, the **bûche de Noël,** an attractive log-shaped cake, heads the pastry list.

Les Panetons

113, rue Mouffetard

Métro line 7, Censier-Daubenton Station

Telephone: 01-47-07-12-08

Open daily, except Monday, from 7:00 A.M. to 8:00 P.M.

This small, busy bakery among the street markets of the crowded rue Mouffetard features **pains de campagne** (country-style breads) and a line of pastries that just won't stop. We tried the **chausson aux pruneaux** (prune-filled pastry) and their **tartes**—fruit pies two inches deep, made with berries, apples, and more. They also make a **fougasse** from shortbread dough.

S.A.R.L. St. Germain

18, blvd. St. Germain

Métro line 10, Maubert-Mutualité Station

Autobus route 86, Cardinal Lemoine Station

Telephone: 01-43-54-44-84

Open daily, except Sunday, from 7:00 A.M. to 8:00 P.M.

A number of special breads are featured in this boulangerie, and the **baguette à l'ancienne** is especially appealing. The display cases are filled with tempting pastries, and there is a coffee bar in the shop where you can enjoy them. Attractions close by are the **Cathédrale de Notre Dame,** just across the Seine, and the **Panthéon,** which is a few blocks south. There is much to see on this famous boulevard.

Steff le Boulanger
(Stéphane Delaunay SA)

123, rue Mouffetard

Métro line 7, Censier-Daubenton Station

Telephone: 01-47-07-35-96

Open daily, except Monday, from 7:00 A.M. to 8:00 P.M. (Sunday
until 2:00 P.M.)

Steff, a pupil of Bernard Ganachaud, opened this shop in 1992. In the bakery, the prestigious "La Flûte Gana" sign and the coveted Meilleur Ouvrier de France Award are on display, and here you can observe the baker at work in an open shop. His bakery is not far from the home of Ernest Hemingway at 74, rue du Cardinal Lemoine.

We especially like the sweet, crown-shaped **kugelhopf** with almonds and raisins, an Alsacian specialty, the **tourte aux épinards** (spinach pie), and, among his breads, **la flûte gana** (a very thin baguette). There is an interesting old church, **St. Médard,** nearby.

"Steff" also has a location in "the Seventh": 54, rue de Sèvres.

SYLVAIN HERVET

69, rue Monge

Métro line 7, Place Monge Station

Autobus route 47

Telephone: 01-43-31-27-36

Open daily, except Monday, from 7:00 A.M. to 8:00 P.M.

In addition to having an endless list of specialties, the "Maison Hervet," founded in 1959, is a major catering service. We sampled their **tuile aux amandes,** a delicious almond cookie, and were also attracted to several varieties of meringue and the **sablé aux noix** (shortbread with nuts). Their bread display is likewise impressive, with forty varieties, including **pain au pavot** (poppy seed bread), **flûte à l'ancienne** (long, hard-crust rolls), **petits pains en animaux divers** (small breads shaped like animals), and **fougasses méridionales** (hearth cakes). The Place Monge market is nearby.

Arrondissement

*F*or the history buff, this arrondissement on the Left Bank offers special charm. Paris's oldest bridge, the Pont Neuf (which means "new bridge"); its oldest theater, the Théâtre Odéon; and its oldest church, the Église St. Germain des Prés, are short walks from the bakeries we have listed. The boulevard St. Michel, a main thoroughfare of the Latin Quarter, is the east boundary of "the Sixth," and to the north, toward the Seine, is the fashionable boulevard St. Germain, lined by cafes, cinemas, and expensive boutiques. Yet, the arrondissement is not on most tour bus routes, probably because the streets between the Jardins du Luxembourg and the Seine are so narrow and crooked that they defy automobiles and buses. They say that Baron Haussmann, who led the program to modernize Paris during the Second Empire, retired before he found a way to demolish and rebuild this medieval tangle. The Jardin du Luxembourg and the Palais du Luxembourg, the French Senate building, within the park, are the commanding, central point of "the Sixth." There are many interesting bakeries in this arrondissement, including Paris's most famous, Poilâne. A half-day visit may not be long enough.

ÉATRIX

42, rue Dauphine

Métro line 10 or 4, Odéon Station

Autobus route 70

Telephone: 01-46-33-98-27

Open daily, except Sunday and Monday, from 8:00 A.M. to 8:00 P.M.

From the Odéon Métro station, two blocks north is the rue Dauphine. At 42, rue Dauphine, is M. Béatrix's extremely interesting bakery. He features a number of special breads but points to his **fougasse** as a favorite. This strange-shaped dough concoction is often found in Paris's boulangeries, but each boulanger creates a distinctive loaf, through his or her choice of herbs, spices, and fillings. You can also buy candy by the piece; **mille-feuille au rhum**, a mouth-watering layered pastry with rum filling; and **éclair au chocolat**.

BEZARD, MICHEL

4, rue des Quatre-Vents
Métro line 10 or 4, Odéon Station
Autobus route 58 or 70
Telephone: 01-43-54-67-05
Open daily, except Sunday, from 7:00 A.M. to 8:30 P.M (Saturday
until noon)

The oldest and largest theater in Paris, **Théâtre Odéon,** founded in 1770, is on the north edge of the **Jardin du Luxembourg,** about two blocks south of the short, narrow rue des Quatre-Vents, where this boulangerie is located—an old, historic section of the city. This boulangerie's display of bread is rated among the best in the area, with the familiar white, soft-centered **pain de mie, pain de seigle, pain complet, pain de son,** and several sizes of **baguettes** as his featured products.

CONTINI, MARC

19, blvd. du Montparnasse
Métro line 10 or 13, Duroc Station
Autobus route 29, 82, 89, or 92
Telephone: 01-45-67-21-36
Open daily, except Monday, from 7:00 A.M. to 8:00 P.M. (Sunday
until 1:00 P.M.)

The Duroc Métro station is in the extreme southwest corner of "the Sixth," and as you walk down the boulevard du Montparnasse toward the **Place du 18 Juin 1940,** you will find M. Contini's white-front boulangerie. It is lo-cated on the same street as the famous Montpar-nasse cafés—the **Dôme,** the **Rotonde,** the **Select,** and the **Coupole**—on the boulevard most often associated with poets, painters, and novelists. If the weather is pleas-ant, M. Contini will have his pastry counter pushed out on the sidewalk, tempting all who pass by. There is plenty in the shop as well. Among his breads we were attracted to the **pain de mie** and the **pain de campagne.** His pas-try line features **tartes aux fraises, aux poires,** and **à la crème** (strawberry, pear, and custard pies).

$\mathcal{G}$AULUPEAU, $\mathcal{J}$. $\mathcal{C}$.

12, rue Mabillon

Métro line 10, Mabillon Station

Autobus route 96

Telephone: 01-43-54-16-93

Open daily, except Monday, from 7:00 A.M. to 8:00 P.M.

M. Jean-Claude Gaulupeau's awning reads, "Salon de Dégustation" (wine tasting), and, "Pâtissier" (pastry chef), but we quickly learned that he also features fifteen varieties of bread—excellent products from the tradi-tional baguette to the brioche—all made from organic flour and fermented for a long time. His **éclairs, petits fours,** and **macarons** are outstanding. The shop also has a salon de thé where you can enjoy your selections. Two famous churches are nearby: Paris's oldest, **St. Germain des Prés,** built in 1163, and **St. Sulpice,** built in 1756.

M. GAUTHIER

101, rue de Rennes

Métro line 4, St. Sulpice Station, or Métro line 12, Rennes Station

Autobus route 83, 94, 95, or 96

Telephone: 01-45-48-35-79

Open daily, except Sunday and Monday, from 7:30 A.M. to 8:00 P.M.

The **Jardin du Luxembourg,** a short walk from this bakery, is undoubtedly the most beautiful concentration of gardens in Paris, suggesting picnic opportunities that are hard to equal. It is said that the gardens employ one gardener per acre to plant and nurture the flowers.

The boulanger's specialties include **pain de son** (bran loaf), **pain de seigle** (rye bread), **pain complet** (wholewheat bread), **pain aux six céréales** (six-grain bread), and **pain au levain** (leavened bread). M. Gauthier also has push-out counters ready to go on any nice day. He stocks jars of **confiture aux griottes,** an interesting Morello cherry jam, to complement his excellent breads.

Gérard Mulot

76, rue de Seine

Métro line 10, Odéon Station or Mabillon Station, or Métro line 4,
   Odéon Station or St. Germain des Prés Station

Telephone: 01-43-26-85-77

Open daily, except Wednesday, from 6:45 A.M. to 8:00 P.M.

This gleaming white boulangerie and pâtisserie is one of
Paris's finest. We toured the working area, down many
stairs to the basement, observing at least fifteen skilled
pâtissiers and boulangers still hard at work on a Saturday
afternoon, some having started their day at 3:30 A.M.
The bread shelves offer a complete selection, with **pain
de seigle aux noix** (rye bread with nuts) and an endless
variety of **petits pains** (dinner rolls) featured. The **financiers** and chocolate, lime, lemon, and strawberry **macarons** are outstanding. The Palais du Luxembourg,
dating to 1623, where the French senate prevails (many
of whose members are customers of M. Mulot), is a short
walk away.

GLARDON, ROGER

72, rue Bonaparte
Métro line 4, St. Sulpice Station
Autobus route 84 or 96
Telephone: 01-43-54-47-77
Open daily, except Tuesday and Wednesday, from 7:30 A.M. to
    7:30 P.M.

In a most interesting section of the arrondissement, on rue Bonaparte, you will find this bakery located between two famous churches—**St. Germain des Prés** and **Église St. Sulpice,** the church with one of the world's largest pipe organs. While the bread display in this bakery is impressive, the featured pastries are what really catch one's eye. Try the house specialty, **tarte normande,** or the **meringue aux amandes** (almond meringue) or **tartelettes à l'orange, au chocolat, et aux noix** (tarts flavored with orange, chocolate, and walnuts).

LIONEL POILÂNE

8, rue du Cherche-Midi
Métro line 10 or 12, Sèvres-Babylone Station
Autobus route 68 or 94
Telephone: 01-45-48-42-59
Open daily, except Sunday, from 7:15 A.M. to 8:15 P.M.

You will have no difficulty locating Lionel Poilâne's boulangerie. Simply follow the crowd on rue du

Cherche-Midi to the line at the small shop, which is built over the ruins of a fourteenth-century Gothic abbey and was once the bakery of master baker Pierre Poilâne, the father of the equally famous bakers, Lionel and Max Poilâne. Your patience will be rewarded with butter cookies as you wait your turn to buy his world-famous **boule,** if not a five-pound loaf, at least a slice or two. Poilâne's bread is also available in over 300 restaurants and at least 600 other shops in Paris and is baked not only at this and his other boulangerie at 45 boulevard de Grenelle in "the Fifteenth" but also in the suburb of Bièvres, where he has twenty-four wood-fired ovens. Do not be misled by this volume. His bread—a thick-crusted sourdough—is still handmade in the old style. By request, you can descend the narrow stone stairs to the basement to marvel at the process by which this bread is made. You will see the wood-fired ovens, well over two centuries old, the long-handled wooden spatulas (peels), and the wicker baskets lined with linen, where the sourdough rises. M. Poilâne's product line also features a delightful **pain aux noix, a pain de seigle, croissants, brioches,** and **petits pains au chocolat** (chocolate rolls). When you have visited Poilâne, you have visited perhaps the most renowned bakery in the world.

ℛÉGALADE

118, blvd. Raspail

Métro line 12, Notre-Dame des Champs Station

Autobus route 58, 68, or 82

Telephone: 01-45-48-68-09

Open daily, except Monday, from 7:30 A.M. to 8:00 P.M.

M. Marcel Branchut is patron (proprietor) at this attractive bakery on busy boulevard Raspail, two blocks west of the **Jardin du Luxembourg.** He features several popular breads—baguettes of various sizes and country-style loaves. He is especially proud of the **délicatesses au chocolat** (chocolate delicacies) in his pastry display, and also in his confiserie (confectionery). Takeout foods are available, and the Luxembourg gardens are nearby. Hope for a clear day for a picnic lunch!

ARRONDISSEMENT

"*T*he Seventh," a fan-shaped arrondissement on the Left Bank, is dominated by Paris's most familiar landmark, the Tour Eiffel. Built in 1889 as the center-piece of the World's Fair celebrating the centennial of the French Revolution, the Tour, at 300 meters in height, was for many years the world's tallest structure. Now it has yielded to higher buildings in the United States and Asia, but its 984 feet still places it in the top ten. It remains an engineering marvel, perfectly maintained. From the top, you have a matchless view of Paris, unfolding in every direction. The experience is more memorable at night, when Paris earns its title: "The City of Lights."

The attractions in this district don't stop with the Tower. There is a park adjacent to the Tower, le Champ de Mars, and the École Militaire, the French military academy, at the south side of the park. The Musée d'Orsay is located in the east quarter, on the Seine. Trea-sures of French art from 1848 through 1914 are kept in the musée, in an amazing transformation of the Gare d'Orsay, an old railway station. You will be fascinated by the monstrous old station clock. At the Esplanade des Invalides, in the center of "the Seventh," you will find a complex of museums, the Église St. Louis, and the tomb of Napoléon, ostentatious by any standard. The Palais Bourbon on the Quai houses the carefully guarded Assemblée Nationale (the French equivalent of the House of Representatives). With its many attractions, the arrondissement still has some narrow, centuries-old streets and no shortage of quality boulangeries.

MANDINE

178, rue de Grenelle

Métro line 8, La Tour Maubourg Station

Telephone: 01-45-51-06-35

Open daily, except Sunday and Saturday afternoons, from
7:15 A.M. to 8:00 P.M.

This bakery stands at the corner of rue de Grenelle and
rue Cler. Its awning reads "Pain à l'Ancienne," and as we
entered, we found that the boulanger did indeed feature
old-fashioned bread. While almost every bake-shop sells
the Paris trademark **baguette**, the one served in this bakery has a particularly chewy crumb. The bakery also has
a display of takeout sandwiches, quiches, crêpes, and pastries. The large **Champ de Mars** park is a short two
blocks away, so why not?

ℬOSQUET

63, ave. Bosquet

Métro line 8, École Militaire Station

Telephone: 01-45-51-75-01

Open daily, except Saturday, from 6:30 A.M. to 8:00 P.M.

At the **Pont de l'Alma** and the **Place de la Résistance,** you will find a major tourist destination, **les Égouts de Paris** (the sewers of Paris). Avenue Bosquet begins at this point, so when you are in this part of "the Seventh," stop by the delightful boulangerie bearing the avenue's name. Try their **pain aux raisins et aux noix** (raisin bread with walnuts), the **galettes au citron** (lemon cookies), and their individual-size quiches.

𝒞HATELAIN

52, rue du Bac

Métro line 12, rue du Bac Station

Telephone: 01-45-48-98-23

Open daily, except Saturday and Sunday, from 7:00 A.M. to
    8:00 P.M.

The **Musée d'Orsay** is a short block from the **Pont Royal** and the rue du Bac, so pay M. Chatelain a visit after you have been to this fabulous gallery in the old railway station. He has a great variety of bread—baguettes and boules—including some small loaves that will encourage you to buy cheese nearby to enjoy with them.

Aux Délices de Sèvres

70, rue de Sèvres

Métro line 10 or 13, Duroc Station

Autobus route 70 or 39

Telephone: 01-47-34-65-00

Open daily, except Monday, from 6:30 A.M. to 9:00 P.M.

On the corner of rue de Sèvres and rue Rousselet, there is a very busy bakery you will not want to miss. They offer a virtual library of breads, and inside they display a large sack of farine (flour) with a sign that reads "Farine de Tradition Française," reminding their customers that their products are made with flour milled by traditional French methods. We discovered a different and delicious **baguette aux olives, croissants aux amandes,** and delightful **meringues.** For lunch try the king-size quiche, three inches high with the diameter of a large pizza. A tourist destination nearby is the **Hôtel des Invalides,** where one can view the tomb of Napoléon.

DUCHESNE, BERNARD

134, rue du Bac

Métro line 10 or 12, rue du Bac Station

Autobus route 70, 94, or 87

Telephone: 01-45-48-94-67

Open daily, except Sunday, from 7:00 A.M. to 7:30 P.M.

When you visit M. Duchesne's shop, you are quite close to the **Bon Marché,** the oldest department store in the city, founded in 1852. M. Duchesne's special breads are numerous: **pain de campagne, pain complet, pain de seigle,** and **bâtard,** a very long, thin baguette. He has takeout foods as well—crêpes, salads, and custards to name a few—and there is a small park in the neighborhood for picnics.

FONTAINE DE MARS

112, rue St. Dominique

Métro line 8, École Militaire Station

Autobus route 69, 42, or 87

Telephone: 01-45-51-31-01

Open daily, except Sunday, from 7:30 A.M. to 8:00 P.M.

M. Duchesne is the maître boulanger (master baker) at this century-old boulangerie close to the fountain for which the shop is named. He lists as his specialties **pain d'épices à l'orange** (an orange-flavored bread with spices) and **baguette de tradition (à l'ancienne).** We also liked his **pain de mie** and his **pain aux cinq céréales** (five-grain bread)—not to mention his **madeleines** (tea cakes) and his **quiches.**

GOULEY, ALAIN

40, rue de Bourgogne

Métro line 13, Varenne Station

Telephone: 01-45-51-24-29

Open daily, except Saturday afternoons and Sunday, from 7:00 A.M. to 8:00 P.M.

You are in a busy part of Paris with the **Assemblée Nationale;** the **Hôtel des Invalides** and its **Église du Dôme,** where Napoléon's tomb is located; and the **Musée Rodin.** A stop by M. Gouley's is indeed convenient. At his bakery you will find friendly directions to the nearby attractions and breads and pastries that are hard to resist. The shop is known for its country-style **baguette paysanne.** Viennese pastries are also featured.

MARIE

111, rue St. Dominique

Métro line 8, École Militaire Station

Autobus route 69

Telephone: 01-45-51-24-47

Open daily, except Saturday and Sunday, from 7:30 A.M. to 7:30 P.M.

This small, busy bakery has a seemingly endless inventory of attractive and interesting breads. Like many bakeries in Paris, they display the "Banette" sign, advertising a high-quality brand of flour with no improvers. Other flours include Banette au seigle royal (rye), Banette au levain (with leavin), Banette complet (whole-wheat), and Banette moisson (wheat and rye). At this bakery, we liked the **pain de seigle** (rye bread), **pain aux six céréales** (six-grain loaf), **pain de son** (bran bread), and **pain complet** (whole-wheat). Viennese pastries are also featured.

Le Pain de Marie

85, rue St. Dominique

Métro line 8, La Tour Maubourg Station, or Métro line 8 or 13,
   Invalides Station

Telephone: 01-45-51-88-77

Open daily, except Sunday, from 7:30 A.M. to 8:00 P.M.

This attractive, small bakery with a pink front and a spotted dog on the sign decorating the front is close to the **Esplanade des Invalides** and not far from the **Tour Eiffel.** They feature a **baguette alliance** (a small baguette), **croissants au chocolat,** and **brioches aux raisins.** Don't overlook the delicious **tartes aux pommes** (apple pies). While we visited the shop, schoolchildren came by to spend their small change—always an added attraction for the visitor.

PANETERIA

31, ave. de la Motte Picquet

Métro line 8, École Militaire Station

Telephone: 01-45-51-53-50

Open daily from 7:00 A.M. to 8:30 P.M.

This broad avenue runs alongside the **Champ de Mars,** the large park by the **Tour Eiffel,** as you approach the Seine. Around the corner is the rue Cler, a merchant street with one of the finest markets in Paris. The sign on this boulangerie tells it all: "Des idées plein les pains" ("Breads full of ideas"). We counted no fewer than twenty varieties. The **pain complet** was especially good, as were the **petits pains.**

POUJAURAN

20, rue Jean-Nicot

Métro line 8, La Tour Maubourg Station

Telephone: 01-47-05-80-88

Open daily, except Sunday, from 8:30 A.M. to 8:30 P.M.

You may see the little blue delivery truck, with a pink sign matching the pink color on the front of this shop, in other parts of the city, but Jean-Luc Poujauran's bakery is on a narrow, out-of-the-way street not far from the **Esplanade des Invalides.** He has a well-deserved reputation for baking a chewy **baguette** that is among the very best in Paris. His **croissant biologique** (organic croissant) and **pain de campagne** are equally good. He came to Paris in 1977 from the west of France, where his father was a baker, and opened this shop. You will find his products excellent and his shop, while small, very interesting, well organized, and well deserving of the must-see list.

ROBINEAU

24, rue Cler

Métro line 8, École Militaire Station or La Tour Maubourg Station

Autobus route 28, 92, or 69

Telephone: 01-47-05-18-93

Open daily, except Monday, from 7:00 A.M. to 8:00 P.M.

This bakery is close to the **Champ de Mars,** the **Tour Eiffel,** and the **École Militaire,** the French national military academy. At Robineau, they sell a vast selection of carry-outs that suggest a picnic in the park: sandwiches, panini, quiches, crêpes. M. Robineau has two interesting specialties—**la quignonnette,** chunks of bread in irregular small loaves, and **le triangle** (a triangular bread). His **fougasse** is excellent, and so is his **pain-surprise garni.** Why not take a chance!

STEFF LE BOULANGER
(DELAUNAY, STÉPHANE)

54, rue de Sèvres

Métro line 10, Vaneau Station

Telephone: 01-47-83-97-12

Open daily, except Sunday, from 7:00 A.M. to 7:30 P.M.

A pupil of the famed maître boulanger Bernard Ganachaud, Steff features **flûte gana,** named for his mentor. You will also find several country loaves—**boule de campagne, grand** and **petit campagne**—and **pain de mie,** the familiar white sandwich loaf with little crust and lots of crumb. There are two parks a short walk away, and takeout food is available here. You will also enjoy visiting Steff's other boulangerie in "the Fifth," at 123, rue Mouffetard, where you can watch this famous baker and his staff at work.

ARRONDISSEMENT

"The Eighth" commands more superlatives than most sections of the city. The Place de la Concorde, infamous during the French Revolution, the Egyptian Obélisque, the Grand Palais, and the Petit Palais dominate the southeast quarter. But more than anything, this arrondissement epitomizes the aesthetic magnificence of urban planning—"picture-postcard Paris." The Champs-Élysées, the grandest avenue of all, ten lanes wide with trees on both sides and the most elegant shops, is on every visitor's itinerary. It is one of twelve symmetrical avenues extending from the Charles de Gaulle-Étoile, which circles the Arc de Triomphe, the world's largest triumphal arch. The Arc de Triomphe, commissioned by Napoléon in 1806, is a universally recognized symbol of France, commemorating its military victories. The Étoile surrounding the Arc was probably, in 1907, the world's first traffic circle. It was named for Général de Gaulle in recent years.

"The Eighth" is also the arrondissement of substantial mansions, many converted to embassies, including the United States Embassy on avenue Gabriel and the official residence of the president of France on the very fashionable rue du Faubourg St.-Honoré.

OHIER

270–272, rue du Faubourg St.-Honoré

Métro line 2, Ternes Station, or Métro line 1, 2, or 6, Charles de
  Gaulle-Étoile Station

Telephone: 01-42-27-45-26

Open daily, except Sunday, from 7:30 A.M. to 8:00 P.M.

The **Parc Monceau,** on the north border of "the Eighth,"
is known to be one of the city's favorite picnic spots, so
you will not be alone if you take carry-outs from the
Boulangerie Cohier to this nearby park. In addition to a
complete line of breads, you will find **éclairs au café ou
au chocolat, charlotte au chocolat ou aux poires** (custard with ladyfingers in either chocolate or pear), and
their own chocolates. There is also a coffee bar inside this
small, yet very nice, shop.

E. FAHY

165, rue du Faubourg St.-Honoré

Métro line 1, George V Station, or Métro line 1, 2, or 6, Charles de
   Gaulle-Étoile Station

Autobus route 22, 52, 43, 83, or 93

Telephone: 01-45-63-34-34

Open daily, except Sunday, from 7:00 A.M. to 7:30 P.M.

The rue du Faubourg St.-Honoré is a window-shopper's
dream and is very much an attraction in itself because
of the many prestigious shops. The bakeries on this
fashionable street are equally attractive. M. Fahy's bakery features forty—yes, forty—varieties of bread and
twenty-five choices of sandwiches. The **viennoiserie tout
au beurre** (Viennese all-butter loaf) is especially good.
This bakery also has a coffee bar, and many salads and
sandwiches are packaged, ready to take with you.

FAUCHON

26, Place de la Madeleine

Métro line 8, 12, or 14, Madeleine Station

Telephone: 01-47-42-60-11

Open daily, except Sunday, from 9:40 A.M. to 7:00 P.M.

While the boulangerie is a big part of this enterprise,
there is much more. Fauchon has maintained its reputation as the best-known food shop in Paris since 1886.

Besides the bakery there is a grocery store, a wine shop, and a pastry shop. Fauchon boasts a selection of over 20,000 items from all over the world; a visit here is indeed a Paris experience. You may just want to browse. In any event, it is well worth a stop. The **Madeleine** is right there, a commanding building constructed in 1764, which has had several functions in the past two centuries.

J. M. FAVREAU

27, blvd. des Batignolles

Métro line 2, Place de Clichy Station or Rome Station

Autobus route 30

Telephone: 01-45-22-73-00

Open daily, except Tuesday, from 7:00 A.M. to 8:30 P.M.

In the northeast quarter of "the Eighth," near the very busy **Place de Clichy,** you will find M. Favreau's boulangerie. He makes bread of every description, including some small round loaves for sampling, and delicious pastries. There are **crêpes au rhum** (rum-flavored crêpes), **financiers** (almond cakes), **tartes aux pommes** (apple pies), quiches of several varieties, and **galettes aux amandes** (almond cookies). Friendly salesladies help schoolchildren select "penny candy."

GUILLON, DOMINIQUE

45, rue de Miromesnil
Métro line 9 or 13, Miromesnil Station
Autobus route 52
Telephone: 01-42-65-56-90
Open daily, except Sunday, from 6:30 A.M. to 8:00 P.M.

You will quickly recognize this attractive boulangerie by the glass etchings on the side panels in front of the shop, next to the Métro stop. We visited late in the day, so the bread inventory was depleted, but earlier there are many varieties available. We were impressed by the several small pastries, even sampling mini **éclairs** and **petits fours.** They also have a takeout restaurant, on the other side of the store, featuring many salads, pâté, eggs, fruit, and more, to go with your purchases from the bakery. The fashionable rue du Faubourg St.-Honoré and the **Palais de l'Élysée,** official residence of the president of France, are in the neighborhood.

LENÔTRE

15, blvd. de Courcelles
Métro line 2 or 3, Villiers Station, or Métro line 2, Monceau Station
Telephone: 01-45-63-87-63
Open daily from 9:00 A.M. to 7:00 P.M.

While a qualification for this directory is an answer "Oui" to the question "Faites-vous le pain vous même?"

(Do you bake the bread on the premises?), we are making an exception with Lenôtre. Its five Paris shops are supplied by a large bakery in the suburb of Plaisir. A cozy neighborhood boulangerie it is not, but as an established, highly regarded business supplying countless satisfied customers with excellent products in immaculately clean, attractive stores, it cannot be denied. The beautiful **Parc Monceau** is nearby, and Lenôtre has everything you need for a picnic lunch. There is no end to the inventory of tempting breads and pastries here or in the other four Paris locations.

44, rue d'Auteuil, 16 ème

48, ave. Victor Hugo, 16 ème

61, rue Lecourbe, 15 ème

121, ave. de Wagram, 17 ème

Au Pain Bien Cuit

111, blvd. Haussmann

Métro line 9 or 13, Miromesnil Station, or Métro line 9, St. Augustin Station

Telephone: 01-42-65-06-25

Open daily, except Sunday, from 7:30 A.M. to 7:30 P.M.

As you approach this bakery at the corner of boulevard Haussmann and rue d'Argenson, you may think it is a toy store with a menagerie displayed in the window. It's a display of giraffes, deer, bears, elephants, and more, all made from bread dough. When you enter, you will see many more bread dough figures, even an Eiffel Tower. These sculptures attract customers and tourists from all over the city. The specialty, however, is their **baguette présidentielle et seigle aux noix et raisins,** for which the boulanger, René-Gérard Saint-Ouen, received top honors at the Hôtel de Ville in March 1997. He also received the Grand Prix de la Baguette, organized by the city of Paris, in 1994, 1995, and 1996. The bakery has a salon de thé, which also serves breakfast and lunch. René-Gérard Saint-Ouen was featured on BBC Television in September 1997, expressing a strong position in favor of the new French government laws regarding bakeries. You will want to add this bakery to your must-see list.

Saint Philippe

73, ave. Franklin D. Roosevelt

Métro line 1 or 9, Franklin D. Roosevelt Station, or Métro line 9, St.
   Philippe-du Roule Station

Telephone: 01-43-59-78-76

Open daily, except Saturday, from 7:30 A.M. to 7:30 P.M.

A few steps north of the **avenue des Champs-Élysées,** on avenue Franklin D. Roosevelt, is a classic boulangerie you will not want to miss. M. Gullian, maître boulanger, produces breads and pastries for a never-ending line of hungry customers. It seems that every worker in this quarter of "the Eighth" chooses Saint Philippe at lunchtime, and for good reason. The selection of chewy

baguettes and mini loaves is hard to beat. There are even "hot dogs." They aren't exactly American style, but they are a tempting combination of sausage and cheese in a bun.

Au St. Honoré

97, rue du Faubourg St.-Honoré

Métro line 9 or 13, Miromesnil Station

Autobus route 80

Telephone: 01-42-66-69-51

Open daily, except Sunday, from 7:00 A.M. to 8:00 P.M.

The **Palais de l'Élysée,** the official residence of the president of France, is just a few steps from this charming old bakery. You will see the tricolor flag and armed guards as you approach. Bakers seem to try to outdo one another in producing the pretzel-shaped **fougasse** every baker has a variation on the filling and the type of dough. The fougasse at this bakery has a record number of herbs, spices, and garnishes; we even detected anchovies. They serve quiches, panini, and pizza too. For dessert don't pass up the **truffes** (truffles). They are among the best.

ARRONDISSEMENT

*T*he ninth arrondissement is called the "Opera," and rightly so. During the modernization of Paris in the nineteenth century, Baron Haussmann's greatest extravagance was the famed Paris Opéra, which dominates "the Ninth's" southern section. When it opened in 1875, the Paris Opéra, created by architect Charles Garnier, was indeed the most lavish, opulent opera house in the world. The neighborhood is also fashionable, with many clothing shops and two of the city's largest department stores, the Printemps and Galeries Lafayettes, and the theater district, with many restaurants and bistros. Dare we forget American Express on rue Scribe?

As one heads north, "the Ninth" becomes less fashionable, through solid residential blocks to Pigalle, Paris's former red-light district. However, as you visit some neighborhoods in Pigalle today, you will be impressed by the trendy shops and fashionable apartments—an effort to upgrade, yet maintain its legendary charms. A major attraction is the Moulin Rouge cabaret (which is actually in "the Eighteenth," across the boulevard de Clichy), made famous by the posters of Toulouse-Lautrec and the music of Offenbach. Several blocks south is the famed Folies Bergères on rue Richer, where the cancan chorus line has attracted Paris visitors for generations. In the center of "the Ninth" is the Église Notre-Dame de Lorette, built in 1836, and close by is a delightful park, the Place St. Georges. We have chosen bakeries in representative neighborhoods. Enjoy the contrasts in this arrondissement.

CARON, JEAN

26, rue du Faubourg Montmartre

Métro line 8 or 9, Rue Montmartre Station

Autobus route 74, 67, or 85

Telephone: 01-47-70-33-70

Open daily, except Wednesday and Thursday, from 7:00 A.M. to
8:00 P.M.

On the rue du Faubourg Montmartre, in the south part of "the Ninth," there are many attractions. The **Folies Bergères** is just around the corner, on rue Richer, and **Le Palace,** a disco, is a few doors from M. Caron's bakery, a charming shop with beamed ceilings and a wood-fired oven in the shop, enabling customers to watch the baking. M. Caron lists his **pain de campagne au levain** and a **baguette biologique** as specialties. We also liked his **gâteau aux fruits** (fruitcake), **crème** (custard), and **quiches.**

CHATEAU, M. ET MME. RENÉ

18, rue des Martyrs
Métro line 12, Notre-Dame de Lorette Station
Autobus route 49
Telephone: 01-48-78-83-91
Open daily, except Wednesday, from 6:45 A.M. to 8:00 P.M.

This attractive corner bakery is close to a church of historical note—**Église Notre-Dame de Lorette,** built in 1836—and up the street, you will find the **Place St. Georges,** a pleasant park, a favorite place for mothers pushing baby carriages. In addition to this bakery's wide assortment of breads, we were tempted by their **charlottes** and **mousses, truffes** (truffles), **tartelettes aux fraises** (strawberry tarts), and **croissants aux amandes et au chocolat** (almond and chocolate croissants).

DANIEL DUPUY

13, rue Cadet
Métro line 7, Cadet Station
Autobus route 32
Telephone: 01-48-24-54-26
Open daily, except Tuesday, from 7:00 A.M. to 8:00 P.M.

Here is a boulanger famous for his two types of baguettes: his **rochetour,** made with natural leaven and hand shaped, and his **pain de campagne,** which comes in several sizes, one weighing over 4 pounds! One of his baguettes, with polka-like square docking on the crust, won second prize in the Grand Prix de la Baguette in 1994. The bakery is especially attractive, with glass panels of wheat outside and inside the shop. The **Square de Montholon** is a few steps away, a likely place for a picnic or snack. North, on the **rue Lafayette,** you will find the **Gare du Nord,** Paris's largest railway station.

Le Grand Opéra

13, rue Mogador

Métro line 7 or 9, Chaussée d'Antin-Lafayette Station

Telephone: 01-45-26-61-97

Open daily, except Sunday, from 10:00 A.M. to 2:00 A.M.

You cannot miss this large boulangerie and restaurant one block north of Paris's famed **Opéra,** serving theater and ballet crowds since 1900. Though their line of breads and pastries is a big part of their business, this is much more than a bakery. They specialize in distinctive pastries, especially the **strudel aux pommes et à la canelle** and four different kinds of **crêpes.** There are many varieties of breads, salads, and cheeses for takeout. The American Express office is in the same neighborhood, on rue Scribe. Two of Paris's largest department stores are a short walk away, on boulevard Haussmann—the **Printemps** and the **Galeries Lafayettes.**

HERMIER, SERGE

10, rue des Martyrs
Métro line 12, Notre-Dame de Lorette Station
Autobus route 49
Telephone: 01-48-78-20-17
Open daily, except Tuesday, from 6:45 A.M. to 8:00 P.M.

The familiar red "Banette" sign is prominently displayed on M. Hermier's boulangerie, which features a number of breads made from farine Banette (Banette flour), a blend of rye and wheat: **Banette moisson,** a special bran loaf; **Banette briare,** an unmolded bread made of brown and rye flour; and **la Banette,** a quality baguette with a good, airy crumb. Ask to sample their six-inch **galettes au chocolat** (chocolate cookies). The neoclassical **Église Notre-Dame de Lorette,** a few steps away, is well worth a stop to see the frescoes and statuary.

HOULBERT, GÉRARD

65, rue des Martyrs
Métro line 2 or 12, Pigalle Station
Telephone: 01-48-78-10-23
Open daily, except Saturday and Sunday, from 7:00 A.M. to
    1:00 P.M. and 3:00 P.M. to 8:00 P.M.

A short block south of the boulevard de Clichy, at the corner of rue des Martyrs and rue Alfred Stevens, you will find M. Houlbert's interesting bakery. We visited here late in the day, too late even for their last baking. The regular customers had nearly depleted the bread supply, but the **pain à la banane** (banana bread) and a few baguettes were left. They also sell tarts, pizza, flan, and meringues. Up the hill from the bakery is a major tour bus stop, the **Moulin Rouge** by the Pigalle Métro station.

ℒAFAYETTE 𝒢OURMET

40, blvd. Haussmann

Métro line 7 or 9, Chaussée d'Antin-Lafayette Station

Telephone: 01-48-74-46-06

Open daily, except Sunday, from 8:45 A.M. to 8:15 P.M.

While the in-store bakery, offering bread made by Lionel Poilâne as well as other breads, in the gourmet section of the huge **Galeries Lafayettes** department store hardly qualifies as a boulangerie, it is listed here as a convenient and interesting place to buy good bread and pastry while shopping in the store, and also as an example of the in-store bakeries you will find in the other major department stores throughout the city—**Printemps, Samaritaine, Bon Marché, BHV,** and **Monoprix.** We cannot list them all here, but this location on boulevard Haussmann, close to the **Opéra** and the **American Express** office, is a convenient example.

𝒧ANDRY

65, rue de Clichy

Métro line 2 or 13, Place de Clichy Station

Telephone: 01-48-74-07-43

Open daily, except Saturday and Sunday, from 7:00 A.M. to
8:00 P.M.

It is a bit confusing to learn that there is a boulevard de
Clichy, an avenue de Clichy and a rue de Clichy, all converging on the Place de Clichy. M. Landry is on the rue,
a busy one-way street running north to the square. There
are discos, theaters, and a casino on this street, as well as
this top-rated bakery with a menu of takeouts to rival
those of the busiest bakeries in the city. The **croque-
monsieur** is a winner, as are the baguettes hot from the
oven and the **galettes** (cookies), pizzas, and quiches.
Mousse au chocolat and **crème caramel** top off the
menu.

ℒETOUZE

71, rue St. Lazare

Métro line 12, Trinité Station

Autobus route 21, 49, or 68

Telephone: 01-48-74-59-52

Open daily, except Saturday and Sunday, from 6:30 A.M. to
7:00 P.M.

From this boulangerie, it is only a short walk to the **Gare St. Lazare,** a major railway station serving the northwest section of Paris, and a beautiful old church, the **Église Trinité,** in the other direction. The **Opéra** and a large department store, the **Galeries Lafayettes,** are within walking distance to the south. Specialties at this boulangerie include a very attractive **tarte normande** and **flan.** You will enjoy the great selection of breads—**pain complet, pain aux cinq céréales,** and **pain de seigle.**

ℳAISON ℱEYEUX

56, rue de Clichy

Métro line 2 or 13, Place de Clichy Station; Métro line 12, Trinité
Station; or Métro line 13, Liège Station

Autobus route 68 or 81

Telephone: 01-48-74-37-64

Open daily, except Monday, from 7:30 A.M. to 7:30 P.M.

Walking south from the noisy **Place de Clichy** on the rue de Clichy, at the corner of rue Cardinal Mercier, you will discover a boulangerie that you will not forget. They offer free samples of quiche and other hot delicacies for everyone, and after a brief break for a snack and coffee at the inside tables, you will be treated to homemade **truffes** (chocolate truffles) that you cannot resist. Two dishes caught our attention: **tourte à l'aubergine,** eggplant pie with potatoes and bacon, and **tourte Picard,** a chicory and chicken tart. Yes, there is also a complete bread display—and desserts! Try the **marquis mousse au chocolat** (imperial chocolate pudding), the flan, and the plum and apple tarts. This is a great stop as you visit the Montmartre section of the city.

ARRONDISSEMENT

*T*wo railway stations and a canal dominate "the Tenth." The Gare du Nord must be the largest of Paris's six rail terminals. Built in 1863, its grandiose exterior is topped with statues representing several larger cities of France. The enormousness of the glass-and-steel parapluie (umbrella) over the train tracks is something to see. Two blocks away is the Gare de l'Est, which is a bit smaller. Another block east is the Canal St. Martin, about three miles long and connected to the Seine. In this section of the city, there are many hotels offering accommodations to thousands of travelers departing from the railway stations. There is even a street named for the many hotels, rue des Petits Hôtels.

Still, there is much more to this district than the rail stations and the canal. East of the canal is one of the city's oldest hospitals, the Hôpital St. Louis. "The Tenth" is also known for its ethnic food markets and restaurants, especially on the rue du Faubourg St. Denis as you walk south to the second arrondissement, and we discovered several very interesting bakeries as we explored "the Tenth."

ERRY

159, rue du Faubourg St. Denis

Métro line 4 or 5, Gare du Nord Station

Autobus route 26, 31, 54, or 65

Telephone: 01-42-82-19-35

Open daily, except Saturday and Sunday, from 6:00 A.M. to
8:30 P.M.

This large corner bakery is within sight of the **Gare du Nord** in a very busy neighborhood, yet we found friendly salespeople who proudly showed us a complete selection of breads, pastries, and takeouts. We liked the **pain aux herbes** (whole-grain bread with herbs) and the **paysanne**, a crusty white bread. They have **galettes au chocolat et aux noix** (chocolate cookies with nuts), tarts, chocolates, and many sandwiches.

Doussoux

112, blvd. de Magenta

Métro line 4 or 5, Gare du Nord Station

Autobus route 30, 35, 56, or 54

Telephone: 01-40-35-76-23

Open daily, except Wednesday, from 7:00 A.M. to 8:00 P.M.

The huge, renovated **Marché St. Quentin,** built in 1866 with a glass ceiling to rival that of the Gare du Nord, is a short block from this small, well-equipped bakery. While the market may have "everything," we suggest M. Doussoux's special breads. We liked the **pain normand,** a loaf from an old Norman recipe, and the **pain aux châtaignes,** a loaf with chestnuts. His line of sweets is outstanding, topped by a chocolate meringue, tarts, and éclairs. He lists as one of his specialties **torréfaction du café** (fresh-roasted coffee).

Gbo Boulangerie

186, rue du Faubourg St. Denis

Métro line 4 or 5, Gare du Nord Station

Autobus route 350 or 65

Telephone: 01-40-37-74-60

Open daily, except Sunday, from 6:30 A.M. to 8:30 P.M. (half day
  on Saturday)

Here is a small, friendly neighborhood bakery in the shadow of the **Gare du Nord,** a quick stop for fresh bread and pastry before you board the train. They feature a great assortment of sandwiches, wrapped and ready to go, quiches, crêpes, and delicate cookies to send you on your way or for you to snack on while waiting for your train.

ℐUILLET

12, rue du 8 Mai 1945

Métro line 4, 5, or 7, Gare de l'Est Station

Autobus route 30, 31, 32, 38, 39, or 65

Telephone: 01-40-35-74-07

Open daily, except Tuesday, from 6:00 A.M. to 7:30 P.M.

This bakery is just across the street from the **Gare de l'Est**, a convenient stop before boarding your train and a chance to pick up snacks and sandwiches for the trip. M. Guillet features a **pain au fromage** (cheese bread) that you will find irresistible. Pastries and chocolates are made in the shop, all delicious: **pâte d'amande aux noisettes** (hazelnut and almond paste), **éclairs au chocolat, mousse à la fraise** (strawberry mousse), and **nougat à la pistache** (pistachio nougat).

ℳAISON 𝒪GER

74, blvd. de Magenta

Métro line 4, 5, or 7, Gare de l'Est Station

Telephone: 01-42-05-39-28

Open daily, except Sunday, from 7:30 A.M. to 8:00 P.M.

With two major rail terminals and more hotels per block than any other arrondissement, there is not much room for bakeries in "the Tenth," but we did discover a few. None is more convenient to the **Gare de l'Est** and the **Gare du Nord** than M. Oger's boulangerie, where you can easily pick up a snack as you head for the train. He features a **baguette viennoise, éclairs** and other custard products, and very good **crêpes.**

𝒯APIAU

83, blvd. Magenta

Métro line 4, 5, or 7, Gare de l'Est Station

Autobus route 30, 31, 32, 38, 39, or 65

Telephone: 01-47-70-31-70

Open daily, except Sunday, from 6:30 A.M. to 8:00 P.M.

Tapiau is a very attractive bakery close to the **Marché St. Quentin** and the **Gare de l'Est.** In addition to a tempting array of breads they have **casse-croûtes** (snacks), ranging from Disney-character candy for children to mouthwatering pastries, and also a vast selection of wine. We were fascinated by an Italian coffee machine steaming espresso.

ARRONDISSEMENT

The boulevard Voltaire, from the Place de la République to the Place de la Nation, bisects this largely residential section of the city. The Place de la Bastille is the site of the prison originally built in the fourteenth century. The Bastille was stormed by revolutionaries on July 14, 1789, and that date is now observed as a major holiday, Bastille Day, La Fête Nationale. Although the old prison was demolished many years ago, remnants of the original foundation are displayed at the Bastille Métro station and are also stacked up as a memorial in the Square Henri Galli, a few blocks down the boulevard Henri IV. Close by the square is the new Opéra Bastille, where the "Eleventh" meets the "Third" and "Twelfth." Here you will also find avant-garde shops, galleries, and trendy nightlife.

ALAIN THUILLET

23, blvd. Voltaire

Métro line 5 or 9, Oberkampf Station

Autobus route 96

Telephone: 01-48-05-81-03

Open daily, except Wednesday, from 7:00 A.M. to 8:30 P.M.

We checked into our apartment Sunday evening with little hope that a store would be open in the neighborhood, so we were pleasantly surprised to discover a light on at M. Thuillet's bakery. We selected a baguette that was crispy on the outside with a chewy honey-colored inside. It was a delightful welcome to Paris on a chilly November night. We made a return visit a few days later, quite early in the morning, to find the shop crowded with eager customers, familiar with his natural breads and other products. He gets an A+ for pastries too, for his **financiers** and **madeleines.** This is a busy neighborhood bakery providing superb products to the area residents.

L'AUTRE BOULANGER (M. COUSIN)

43, rue de Montreuil

Métro line 1, 2, or 6, Nation Station; Métro line 8, Faidherbe
Chaligny Station; or Métro line 9, Boulets Montreuil Station

Telephone: 01-43-72-86-04

Open daily, except Saturday afternoon and Sunday, from 7:30 A.M.
to 1:30 P.M. and from 4:00 P.M. to 7:30 P.M.

With a strong recommendation from the nearby hotel
staff, we waited until 4:00 P.M. to enjoy this exception-
ally good boulangerie midway between the **Place de la
Nation** and the **Place de la Bastille.**

From the beam-ceilinged shop you can see the wood-
fired oven and the working area. The shop's stone walls
are a mini museum of bakery artifacts—hats, baskets,
wheels, baking pans, etc. They make a special Italian
bread, **ciabatta,** and two other distinctive loaves—the
rustical and the **nordländer.** You will also like the
brioche with Emmenthal cheese and a **fougasse** with
olives, onions, bacon, or "you name it."

À LA BONNE BAGUETTE

144, blvd. Voltaire

Métro line 9, Voltaire Station

Autobus route 46 or 56

Telephone: 01-42-63-34-52

Open daily, except Sunday, from 7:00 A.M. to 8:00 P.M.

Featured items include country-style baguettes and a complete line of pastries. The **tartelettes aux fraises et au citron** (strawberry and lemon tarts) are very attractive, and their **flan, chocolat aux noix,** and trays of ham-and-cheese sandwiches are tempting. There are tables and chairs out front where you can relax and enjoy lunch.

$\mathscr{B}$OULANGER $\mathscr{M}$ICHEL

103, ave. Parmentier

Métro line 3, Parmentier Station

Autobus route 46

Telephone: 01-43-57-53-27

Open daily, except Sunday, from 7:00 A.M. to 8:30 P.M.

At the corner of avenue Parmentier and rue des Trois Bornes, across the street from another fine boulangerie—Poitrimoult—you will find Boulanger Michel. The fascinating glass decorations on the outside give the shop an ancient appearance, while the inside of the shop is quite modern and bright. Michel features some unusual breads—**pain aux châtaignes** (chestnut bread); **pain paysan,** a rustic peasant loaf; **pain italien; pain antique;** and **pain aux six céréales,** a healthy loaf. He also has an interesting display of pastries—apricot, apple, rhubarb, strawberry, and lemon tarts—and a novelty, a small pink pig! Michel told us that he uses floral decorations on bread and offers hot plate lunches.

A. CHAINEAU

28, blvd. Beaumarchais
Métro line 5, Bréguet-Sabin Station
Telephone: 01-47-00-17-56
Open daily, except Wednesday, from 7:00 A.M. to 8:00 P.M.

You will recognize A. Chaineau's shop by its blue, quaintly decorated front. It is located in the south quarter of "the Eleventh," close to the **Place de la Bastille** and the **Place des Vosges,** Paris's oldest public square, surrounded by charming sixteenth-century townhouses. M. Chaineau's specialties range from a very crusty baguette to an extensive line of pastries, sandwiches, and chocolates.

M. COCHEREL

121, rue de Charonne
Métro line 9, Charonne Station
Autobus route 76
Telephone: 01-43-71-33-06
Open daily, except Tuesday and Wednesday, from 6:30 A.M. to
8:15 P.M.

Specialties include a six-grain bread without rye, a **pain de mie** that is nearly all interior crumb and has very little crust, and **brioche.** You will also find tempting sandwiches for takeout and irresistible homemade **truffes.**

DANIEL MORIN

135, rue de Charonne
Métro line 9, Charonne Station
Autobus route 76
Telephone: 01-43-71-45-21
Open daily, except Sunday and Monday, from 6:30 A.M. to 8:30 P.M.

Located on the corner of rue de Charonne and rue Léon Frot is this most interesting bakery. We found many traditional breads and beautiful pastries. We sampled **armande**, an almond pastry, and their **tarte aux pommes vertes** (green apple pie). For takeout, try the **Morin mousse au chocolat!**

FÉRET, DIDIER

149, rue du Faubourg Saint-Antoine
Métro line 8, Ledru-Rollin Station
Autobus route 86
Telephone: 01-43-46-02-08
Open daily, except Sunday, from 7:00 A.M. to 8:00 P.M.

This appears to be a small and ordinary bakery, but wait until you go inside and see the beamed ceiling and tile floor. M. Féret's **pain de campagne** is crusty and very good, as is his **baguette viennoise.** We also liked his blueberry, fig, and almond **tartelettes** and the many tempting items for lunch in the park nearby. There is a

Monoprix at the Métro stop, where you can buy the rest of your picnic menu. The **Place de la Bastille** is about three blocks west.

A. Hort

182, blvd. Voltaire

Métro line 9, Voltaire Station

Autobus route 46 or 56

Telephone: 01-43-71-33-11

Open daily, except Saturday, from 6:30 A.M. to 8:15 P.M. (half day on Sunday)

We were attracted to their wide variety of breads, from a large **boule** to an extra-long **baguette** and a country-style **campagne**. M. Hort's shop is a great place for lunch, with many sandwiches ready to go, quiches, salads, and even "hot dogs with cheese." We were intrigued by the **tartelette au saumon frais et aspèrges** (salmon with asparagus, an open-face sandwich).

J. ODIER

136, rue de la Roquette

Métro line 9, Voltaire Station (Léon Blum)

Autobus route 61 or 69

Telephone: 01-43-79-65-98

Open daily, except Monday and Tuesday, from 6:30 A.M. to 8:00 P.M.

This bakery offers a great variety of special breads, **campagne, seigle aux noix, baguette aux raisins,** mouthwatering **pudding au chocolat avec noix** (chocolate pudding with walnuts), **flan, tartes aux abricots** (apricot pies), and especially **couronne pâte à chou,** a ring of flavored pastries. These folks also make their own chocolate.

POITRIMOULT, GILLES ET FLORENCE

101, ave. Parmentier

Métro line 3, Parmentier Station

Autobus route 46

Telephone: 01-47-00-23-31

Open daily, except Monday, from 7:30 A.M. to 8:15 P.M.

We have seen many outside glass panels with interesting farm and wheat scenes, but this corner boulangerie displaying the Banette sign has some of the most charming panels we have seen. The complete line of Banette breads is available here, in addition to a tempting variety of takeout snacks. Their **quiche au lard et au thon** (bacon and tuna quiche) and the **croissant au jambon** (ham croissant) are exceptional. You will also find several dainty pastries—**opéra, tartelettes** of many varieties, and more.

ROBERT, PASCAL

28, blvd. Voltaire

Métro line 5 or 9, Oberkampf Station

Autobus route 56 or 96

Telephone: 01-47-00-45-17

Open daily, except Sunday, from 6:45 A.M. to 8:00 P.M.

As you visit this fascinating bakery, you are quite close to the **Place de la République** and not far from the **Bastille.** Specialties include **pain biologique** (organic bread), chocolate delicacies, flan, and a complete array of sandwiches for takeout to a nearby pocket park.

ARRONDISSEMENT

*B*y every measurement, you are visiting the genuine Paris when you visit "the Twelfth." In the north corner, where "the Twelfth" meets "the Fourth" and "the Eleventh," you will find the Opéra Bastille. Conceived as "The People's Opera House" as a major project of the late President Mitterrand, it was inaugurated on Bastille Day 1989. With over one million spectators each year and attractions generally less expensive than at the historic Paris Opéra, it has made its mark. In fact, it has supplanted the Paris Opéra. The Opéra Bastille is now the only place to see opera in Paris. The old opera house now presents only ballet.

At the opposite end of the arrondissement is the Bois de Vincennes, noted for the Lac Daumesnil and the Parc Zoologique (the zoo). The Gare de Lyon, the rail terminal for trains headed south, is just a block from the Seine on the west side, and the monstrous arena, the Palais Omnisports de Paris-Bercy, is close to the river, at Pont de Bercy. Besides all these attractions, "the Twelfth" is a fascinating composite of neighborhoods, some upscale but most with comfortable, modest apartments.

ℬAZIN, ℐACQUES

85, bis rue de Charenton

Métro line 8, Ledru-Rollin Station

Telephone: 01-43-07-75-21

Open daily, except Wednesday and Thursday, from 7:00 A.M. to
8:00 P.M.

M. Bazin's boulangerie has the enthusiastic recommendation of several police officers with whom we visited on this corner, and you will be likewise impressed. The boulanger likes to add nuts to his rye breads—hazelnuts, almonds, walnuts—and often raisins. Another specialty is his **pain bûcheron** (woodcutter bread), a mixture of whole wheat and rye. We even detected sunflower seeds. The very modern **Opéra de Paris-Bastille** is a short walk up rue de Charenton. This nineteenth-century boulangerie will feel like a trip back in time for any "bakery sleuth."

BISSON, CLAUDE

4, rue du Général-Leclerc (Charenton)

Métro line 8, Charenton-Écoles Station

Autobus route 24, 111, or 325

Telephone: 01-43-68-83-03

Open daily, except Wednesday and Tuesday afternoon, from
6:00 A.M. to 11:15 A.M. and from 2:30 P.M. to 8:00 P.M.

If you continue south on rue du Général-Leclerc, you will be in the **Bois de Vincennes,** one of Paris's four largest parks, with a lake, a zoo, and other attractions. Actually, M. Bisson's boulangerie is jut beyond the twelfth arrondissement and is our only listing outside of Paris's corporate limits. We did, however, have a good reason to stray beyond the city limits. Our destination was the **Musée Français du Pain.** We found the address—25, bis rue Victor-Hugo, in Charenton-le-Pont—but the gate was locked, since the museum had closed two years before! Nevertheless, we discovered a very friendly bakery, and a park just a few steps away. You will enjoy their **brioche;** it's higher and flakier than most. And in the pastry display they have **macarons** in several colors and flavors. They also have a sidewalk ice cream stand in front of the shop.

ℬoulangerie 𝒜nne 𝒥amet

57, ave. du Docteur Arnold Netter

Métro line 1, 2, 6, or 9, Nation Station, or Métro line 6, Picpus
    Station

Autobus route 62

Telephone: 01-43-43-91-73

Open daily, except Wednesday, from 7:15 A.M. to 8:00 P.M.

You will find many interesting breads at this modern corner bakery. Her specialties are not confined to the hearty, whole-grain loaves, but there are several—**pain paysan, pain forestier, pain aux céréales, pain complet.** The **pain de mie,** the white sandwich-type bread, is especially good, as is the **baguette au levain naturel** (naturally leavened baguette). For dessert try the **pâte de fruit aux mûres,** a mulberry pie with a superb flaky crust. An added attraction is a collection of clown dolls. We did not ask, but the chances are they are for sale. If not, they are delightful to look at.

LA CHOCOLATINE

100, rue Claude Decaen

Métro line 6 or 8, Daumesnil Station

Autobus route 46

Telephone: 01-46-28-03-25

Open daily, except Sunday, from 6:30 A.M. to 8:30 P.M.

We were attracted to this bakery by the large bouquet of yellow flowers in a blue vase in the window. With a bakery named Chocolatine, M. and Mme. Agis make it very hard to pass them by. They do have chocolate, but they also have a variety of **tartelettes aux fraises** and **délices aux fruits** (strawberry and fruit tarts). Their **fougasse** is something special. You will find this boulangerie close to the busy **Place Félix Éboué.**

CROSNIER

62, rue de Reuilly

Métro line 6, Dugommier Station

Autobus route 29

Telephone: 01-43-44-55-37

Open daily, except Wednesday, from 6:45 A.M. to 8:00 P.M.

This boulangerie is in the neighborhood of the Place de la Nation, where nine streets converge at the boundary between "the Eleventh" and "the Twelfth." Students of the French Revolution will tell you that a guillotine responsible for over 1,300 severed heads was located here. The

Boulangerie Crosnier is a few short blocks south, and you will find a great inventory of traditional breads, all products of an artisan baker. The **boule paysanne** (country-style round loaf), **pain aux noix** (nut bread), and **pain au sésame** (sesame-topped bread) all attracted our attention.

ℒℯ ℭʏɢɴℯ 𝒟ᴏʀᴇ́ (I. & L. GOMES)

219, ave. Daumesnil

Métro line 6 or 8, Daumesnil Station

Autobus route 46

Telephone: 01-43-07-81-93

Open daily, except Wednesday, from 6:30 A.M. to 8:15 P.M.

This was our neighborhood boulangerie, next door to our apartment building, so we saw it often. There is a continuous line of customers eager to buy the Gomeses' excellent Banette breads and pastries. Their **pain de seigle** and **pain de son** are excellent. We also like their **pain aux raisins**. It's chock-full of raisins. They also sell **salades de tomates et épinards** (tomato and spinach salad) and other attractive takeouts. You will not forget their **gâteau au chocolat,** a chocolate cake for the memory book. Look for the blue bakery on the corner, with the red Banette sign.

DEROUVILLE, SERGE

195, rue de Charenton
Métro line 6, Dugommier Station
Autobus route 29
Telephone: 01-43-43-59-14
Open daily, except Saturday and Sunday, from 6:30 A.M. to 8:00 P.M.

This appealing bakery on rue de Charenton, just down the street from the Mairie du XII (the town hall for "the Twelfth"), sports the familiar blue decal designating an artisan boulanger. M. Derouville offers a complete line of breads, yet lists as his specialties several mouthwatering pies—**tarte normande, tarte paysanne, tarte lorraine,** and a **tarte à la rhubarbe** we could not resist. We also liked his crêpes, cheese croissants, and quiches, and he receives special mention because he has "penny candy" for the children.

FREUSLON, ROGER

83, ave. du Docteur Arnold Netter
Métro line 1, Porte de Vincennes Station
Telephone: 01-43-07-67-48
Open daily, except Monday, from 7:00 A.M. to 8:00 P.M. (Sunday until noon)

With its beamed ceiling, two ovens built into an interior stone wall, and an endless queue of customers extending into the street, this is a premier boulangerie. Upon viewing and sampling the products, you will not be disappointed. M. Freuslon offers several **demi-pains,** convenient half loaves of **bâtards** and **baguettes,** along with a very attractive **pain de campagne au levain naturel.** He also features **ficelle** and **pain épi.** There are pastries and confections, too, and a park nearby in which to relax and enjoy your purchase.

LEPONT, J.Y.

102, rue du Faubourg Saint-Antoine

Métro line 8, Ledru-Rollin Station

Autobus route 86, 76, or 61

Telephone: 01-43-07-44-25

Open daily, except Saturday and Sunday, from 7:00 A.M. to 8:00 P.M.

You will discover a more complete assortment of bread than the rather nondescript exterior of this bakery suggests: the **pain bâtard,** a wheat bread about the weight of a baguette; an attractive **pain de seigle; pain complet;** and a short loaf called **pain parisien.** M. Lepont has some appealing sweet concoctions too. You will like his **gâteau aux pommes** (apple cake) and **flan naturel,** the custard found everywhere in Paris. There are also apricot, apple, and plum tarts, **éclairs,** and **financiers.** You are not far from the **Opéra de Paris-Bastille.**

Moisan: Le Pain au Naturel

5, Place d'Aligre

Métro line 8, Ledru-Rollin Station

Telephone: 01-43-45-46-60

Open daily, except Sunday and Monday, from 8:00 A.M. to
1:30 P.M. and from 3:30 P.M. to 8:00 P.M.

M. Michel Moisan's new location is easy to find, across
the street from the popular **Marché de Beauvau St.
Antoine.** You will be attracted to his two sales counters:
one sells the standard breads—**baguettes** and the traditional **flûte,** among others—and the other sells the
organic breads from stone-ground flour. He specializes in
pain biologique, only the finest products from natural
ingredients.

S.N.C. des Boulangeries du P.L.M.

1, rue Michel-Chasles

Métro line 1 or 14, Gare de Lyon Station

Autobus route 57, 63, or 91

Telephone: 01-43-43-39-80

Open daily, except Sunday, from 7:00 A.M. to 8:00 P.M. (Saturday
until noon)

This bakery is located one block north of the **Gare de
Lyon,** a major railway terminal that serves not only the
SNCF (major French railroads) but the R.E.R.
(Regional Express Line). From there you can take the A4

to Disney Paris. The gérant (manager) of the boulangerie is M. Guy Avisse, who proudly points to several distinctive breads as his specialties. We liked his **baguette de campagne et aux céréales** and **pain de campagne au seigle.** He also has sandwiches wrapped and ready for passengers heading for the nearby rail station.

S.N.C. Courteline

66, blvd. Picpus

Métro line 6, Picpus Station

Autobus route 59 or 26

Telephone. 01-43-43-67-10

Open daily, except Tuesday, from 6:45 A.M. to 8:00 P.M.

Not far from the **Place de la Nation** is a modern bakery with many very tempting items. With an attractive array of fifteen different breads we chose the **pain brioché.** The egg-enriched yeast bread oozing in butter was not on our diet, but it was oh so good! The **feuilleté,** a puff cream pastry with almonds, and the apple, chocolate, and mixed fruit **tartes** are delicious.

VAUTIER, PIERRE

239, rue de Charenton
Métro line 6, Dugommier Station, or Métro line 6 or 8, Daumesnil
   Station
Autobus route 69 or 87
Telephone: 01-43-07-62-70
Open daily, except Monday, from 6:00 A.M. to 8:30 P.M.

M. Vautier has several **spécialités viennoises** (Viennese specialties), a reminder that the familiar baguette is actually a French adaptation of a Viennese loaf. His **financiers** (almond cakes) are some of the most attractive we have seen, and his **croissants au jambon** (ham sandwiches on croissants) are delicious. He proudly tells us that all his products are made on the premises.

ARRONDISSEMENT

The Seine is the east boundary of "the Thirteenth," with the Gare d'Austerlitz in the extreme northeast corner and a major hospital complex, the Hôpital de la Pitié-Salpétrière, close by. Facing the river is the recently opened French national library, la Grande Bibliothèque de France, reputed to have the largest collection in Europe. The south boundary of the arrondissement is the boulevard Périphérique and a number of parks and recreational areas. Most tourists identify "the Thirteenth" with Chinatown and its growing population of many Asian nationalities. The Place d'Italie, with an abundance of exotic shops, cafés, groceries with ethnic foods, and restaurants, is the starting point for exploration of these neighborhoods. A major historical stop is the Manufacture des Gobelins, where skilled artisans weave tapestries as their predecessors have since 1663. While tours are still possible, many of the valuable tapestries can be seen at the Musée Cluny in the Latin Quarter. While this arrondissement is largely residential, dominated by working-class tenants, many in high-rise apartments, it also has a number of office buildings and some very interesting bakeries.

COLLE, ÉRIC

5, blvd. du Port-Royal

Métro line 7, Les Gobelins Station

Autobus route 91

Telephone: 01-43-37-95-92

Open daily, except Monday, from 7:00 A.M. to 8:00 P.M.

M. Colle's boulangerie is at the intersection of boulevard Arago and boulevard du Port-Royal. His special breads are a **baguette de campagne** (country-style baguette), a **pain fagot** ("poor man's" bread), and the **baguette du patron** (the manager's choice). His candy selection is noteworthy too. We sampled his **pralines au chocolat.**

GUYARD

5, blvd. Arago

Métro line 7, Les Gobelins Station

Autobus route 83 or 91

Telephone: 01-47-07-52-61

Open daily, except Tuesday, from 7:00 A.M. to 8:00 P.M.

Quite close to Éric Colle's boulangerie is another very attractive shop, Guyard. We counted seventeen varieties of bread, all baked on the premises by an artisan boulanger. While all the breads are attractive, we especially remember his buttery **brioche à l'oeuf.** It is hard to turn down his **cheesecake** and **financiers.** They have sandwiches and quiches of several recipes, and both the cheese and the spinach quiches are particularly appetizing. There is a Monoprix supermarket down the street, where you can pick up anything else you need for lunch in a nearby park.

L'HERMINE

114, rue de Patay

Métro line 6, Nationale Station

Autobus route 27 (rue de Patay)

Telephone: 01-45-83-80-13

Open daily, except Wednesday, from 6:00 A.M. to 8:00 A.M.

The famous **Église Jeanne d'Arc** is very close to Madame l'Hermine's delightful bakery, and a small park is just a block or so away. Her bread may be purchased at two separate sales counters: one for traditional breads, the other for whole-grain, organic loaves. You will like her **tous les pains biologiques,** the wholly organic bread that she lists as one of her specialties. There is also a tempting display of takeout foods for a picnic in the nearby park. The new **Bibliothèque de France** is in this general area, and across the Seine is the extensive **Parc de Bercy** and an adjoining sports complex.

𝓜INZIÈRE

123, rue Léon Maurice Nordmann

Métro line 6, Glacière Station, or Métro line 7, Les Gobelins Station

Autobus route 21 or 83

Telephone: 01-47-07-12-78

Open daily, except Sunday and Monday, from 7:30 A.M. to
1:30 P.M. and from 4:00 P.M. to 8:00 P.M.

The rue de la Santé and a large prison, the **Maison d'Arrêt de la Santé,** mark the boundary with "the Fourteenth." M. Minzière's bakery is just one block away. The familiar Banette sign is displayed, assuring us of a complete line of breads. The **Banette fibre,** a long, pointed, high-fiber baguette, was one of our favorites. They sell **tartelettes au caramel et aux noix** (tarts with nuts and caramels) and a meringue with burnt-almond custard. We also remember their **croustades aux champignons** (small pastries with mushrooms) and their **sablés aux noix.** Muffins are not as common in Paris as in New York, but here we found some with chocolate and fruit— **petits pains ronds au chocolat et aux fruits.**

𝒫LANE, 𝒫AUL

53, bis blvd. Arago

Métro line 6, Glacière Station

Telephone: 01-47-07-14-58

Open daily, except Wednesday and Thursday, from 7:30 A.M. to
2:00 P.M. and from 4:00 P.M. to 8:00 P.M.

The northwest corner of "the Thirteenth" is the location of several prominent hospitals: the **Hôpital Péan** and the **Hôpital Militaire,** with others on the east side, by the **Gare d'Austerlitz.** This small bakery, located in that area, features one of the finest Alsacian crown-shaped **kugelhopfs** that we found in Paris. They also have an interesting **pain au levain** and some crunchy **petits pains.**

𝒮t. 𝒯UFFIER (M. PUIVIF)

1, rue du Docteur Tuffier

Métro line 7 or 14, Maison Blanche Station

Telephone: 01-45-88-62-88

Open daily, except Wednesday and Thursday, from 7:00 A.M. to
8:00 P.M.

This bakery is in a most interesting section of "the Thirteenth," with **le Quartier Chinois** ("Chinatown") occupying several blocks close to M. Puivif's bakery. There are many Chinese, Vietnamese, Cambodian, and other Asian restaurants and shops in the area. At the south border of the arrondissement, a short walk from the bakery, is the **Parc Kellermann,** with an interesting medieval gate. Bread is definitely the specialty of M. Puivif's bakery, with an abundance on display: the familiar white **pain de mie,** a hearty **pain de campagne, pain de seigle, pain de son,** and **pain complet.** There are more breads, all appealing.

J. C. VANDERSTICHEL

31, blvd. Arago

Métro line 6, Glacière Station, or Métro line 7, Les Gobelins Station

Autobus route 83

Telephone: 01-47-07-26-75

Open daily, except Sunday, from 6:30 A.M. to 8:00 P.M.

You will recognize this small, very attractive corner bakery by the Dutch windmill decorative glass panel on the front and a shock of wheat by an old oven in another display around the corner. You are sure to meet the patron, whose roots are in Holland. For classic baguettes and **ficelles,** routinely out of the oven late in the morning, it is worth the trip. A house specialty is **pain complet biologique,** an organic loaf, and you will not forget his **pain de campagne.** And he makes beautiful pastries, notably the scallop-shaped **madeleines** and the **pralines au nougat.** And his tarts, puddings, and flans are mouthwatering.

ARRONDISSEMENT

$\mathscr{J}$f the visitor to Paris seeks a composite of the business, cultural, and ethnic lifestyles representing many facets of the city, "the Fourteenth" should be the destination. In the northwest corner is the Tour Montparnasse, claimed by both "the Fourteenth" and "the Fifteenth." With the traffic at the big Gare Montparnasse and tour buses at the fifty-nine-story Tour Montparnasse, this is one of the busiest sections of the city. At the opposite corner, to the southeast, is the Parc Montsouris, begun in 1867 by the renowned Baron Haussmann. It is a sanctuary for many birds, has clearly labeled trees and flowers, and is often crowded with students from the Cité Universitaire close by. This arrondissement also has a cemetery of note, the Cimetière du Montparnasse, where the free *Index des Célébrités* will direct you to the graves of Guy de Maupassant, Samuel Beckett, Jean-Paul Sartre, André Citroën, Alfred Dreyfus, and many other notables. On the east side of "the Fourteenth" is the Hôpital Ste. Anne, a psychiatric hospital first opened in 1221 in the rural environs of the capital. The neighborhoods have attracted immigrants from the rural regions of France and other European countries and would-be writers and artists from America and elsewhere. "The Fourteenth" is a most interesting cross-section of Paris, and not without some authentic boulangeries. Enjoy!

CHENU, JEAN-PIERRE

85, rue Raymond-Losserand
Métro line 13, Pernety Station
Autobus route 28 or 62
Telephone: 01-45-43-28-09
Open daily, except Monday, from 6:30 A.M. to 8:00 P.M.

This busy bakery is on the corner of rue Raymond-Losserand and rue de Plaisance, just one short block from the Pernety Métro station. We were impressed by their complete line of Banette breads: **Banette pain sportif,** a high-energy protein loaf, **Banette complet,** and more. They also have many delicious pastries, with **tartelettes au citron** (lemon tarts), **savarin** (a round, hollow cake), quiches, and meringues. For takeout we recommend the **croissant au jambon,** an open-faced ham sandwich on a croissant. They also make their own chocolates.

CNUDDE, GÉRARD

43, rue Daguerre

Métro line 4 or 6, Denfert-Rochereau Station (also R.E.R., B line)

Autobus route 38 or 68

Telephone: 01-43-22-27-24

Open daily, except Tuesday and Wednesday, from 7:00 A.M. to 8:30 P.M.

You cannot miss this bright red boulangerie at the corner of rue Daguerre and rue Danville. You can watch the bakers at work from the sales area or through an outside window—always an attraction. From the outside window you can observe both the bakers on the first floor and also those working in the basement area. The decor is modern and very attractive. We counted fifteen varieties of bread, including their specialties—**Banette levain, Banette moisson,** and **Banette fibre.** They also make a **pain de mie** and a **petit pain au gruyère,** a small loaf loaded with delicious gruyère cheese. For takeout they have **crudités au thon ou au poulet** (tuna or chicken with raw vegetables) and baguette sandwiches with ham and cheese.

DEPUIS, MICHEL

47, ave. du Maine

Métro line 6, Montparnasse Station, or Métro line 13, Gaîté Station

Autobus route 28 or 58

Telephone: 01-43-20-81-09

Open daily, except Monday and Tuesday, from 7:00 A.M. to 8:00 P.M.

M. Depuis's boulangerie is located on one of the main arteries of "the Fourteenth," quite close to the **Tour Montparnasse** and the railway station. Don't be confused. It's at the corner of rue du Maine and avenue du Maine! M. Dupuis lists peasant and country-style breads as his specialties—**pain paysan** and **pain des bois**—in addition to a circular **couronne de campagne.** His candy selection is extensive, including **rocher aux amandes** (almond cluster), **barres au coco** (coconut bars), and many varieties of chocolate.

L'ÉPI-GAULOIS

23, bis blvd. Brune

Métro line 13, Porte de Vanves Station

Telephone: 01-45-39-34-18

Open daily, except Saturday, from 7:30 A.M. to 8:30 P.M. and
    Sunday from 9:00 A.M. to 2:00 P.M.

This boulangerie does not bake baguettes—quite a distinction in Paris. Their specialty is **pain de campagne,** in many shapes and sizes. Their **couronne,** giant-size and doughnut-shaped, is an interesting and tasty country-style bread. They make **croissants** of several sizes, and the usual **croissant beurre** (croissant with butter) was a bit more expensive. Why not indulge? Croissants back home will never compare. They make **chaussons aux pommes** (apple-filled turnovers), **tartelettes aux mirabelles** (yellow plum tarts), and many other pastries. There are extensive park areas a block south.

Au Fournil de la Gaîté

49, rue de la Gaîté

Métro line 13, Gaîté Station, or Métro line 6, Edgar Quinet Station

Autobus route 58

Telephone: 01-43-22-93-94

Open daily, except Saturday and Sunday, from 6:45 A.M. to 8:30 P.M.

Two blocks from the **Tour Montparnasse** and less than that from the Cimetière du Montparnasse, we chanced upon this cheerful, very neat bakery displaying a red and gold sign reading, "Baguepi." The artisan boulanger is especially proud of his **baguette à l'ancienne** and **pain rustique.** He also features some delightful pastries, particularly the **pavé du roi** and **royal gaîté,** and several kinds of tarts, quiches, and cookies. They also make a spinach-and-cheese concoction that is unique and delicious.

ℒEBLONDEL

96, rue Raymond-Losserand

Métro line 13, Pernety Station

Autobus route 62

Telephone: 01-45-43-42-45

Open daily, except Monday, from 7:00 A.M. to 8:00 P.M.

M. Leblondel displays the blue artisan bakery sign on his shop, where you can actually see the baking operation from the front of the store. He notes his specialties as **classiques,** and we find them classic, traditional, and indeed, very appealing. He offers an array of sandwiches, and there is a park nearby, with a Monoprix on the way—everything you need for a picnic.

ℳAISON ℳÉLI
(LE RENDEZ-VOUS GOURMAND)

4 Place Constantin Brancusi

Métro line 13, Gaîté Station

Autobus route 28

Telephone: 01-43-21-76-18

Open daily, except Monday, from 6:30 A.M. to 8:00 P.M. and
Sunday from 7:00 A.M. to 2:00 P.M.

The familiar blue sign designating an authentic boulanger always attracts us. There are many tables in front of this charming bakery situated at the far end of the Place Constantin Brancusi, with park benches close by, should all the Méli's tables be taken. M. Méli has recently opened this shop, after serving as the chief chef at La Durée, one of the top Parisian tea salons and pastry shops. We visited with a customer who manages a nearby hotel, who recommended Méli's **macarons** as the "best in Paris." They are made in six colors and flavors (vanilla, chocolate, caramel, pistachio, strawberry, and praline) and filled with chocolate or mocha—superb! His specialties include **baguette de farine, pain intégral, baguette biologique, pain aux huit céréales** (a genuine health loaf), and **pain au gruyère.** There are tables inside too; this is a full-scale lunch stop, with a menu of pizza, quiches, panini sandwiches, and salads. Enjoy!

ℳARCHAND

109, ave. du Maine
Métro line 13, Gaîté Station
Autobus route 28 or 58
Telephone: 01-43-22-23-07
Open daily from 3:30 A.M. to 9:30 P.M.

Here is a boulangerie for the early riser; the shop opens when the boulangers arrive for work at 3:30 A.M. Again you can see the bakers working as you check out the extensive display of bread and pastries. They have boules and baguettes of every size, baked to the highest standards. Their selection of tarts—**tartelettes au citron, à l'orange, à la fraise, à la banane** (lemon, orange, strawberry, banana)—is among the best, and we also liked the **tartelettes de nègre praline,** a dark, burnt-almond pastry, and the **tartelettes de nègre chocolat,** a dark-chocolate pastry. This boulangerie is located at the corner of avenue du Maine and rue Daguerre, one block from the **Cimetière du Montparnasse.**

Max Poilâne

29, rue de l'Ouest

Métro line 13 or 6, Montparnasse Station, or Métro line 13, Gaîté Station

Telephone: 01-43-27-24-91

Open daily, except Sunday, from 8:30 A.M. to 7:30 P.M.

Max Poilâne's daughter Sophie presides at this charming, old-fashioned boulangerie in the busy, modern neighborhood of the **Gare Montparnasse.** This is a recommended stop for a snack before you board the train. What can be better than a sandwich made with the famous **pain Poilâne?** Sophie also has an interesting line of jams, gourmet gifts, and candies.

Le Moulin de la Vierge

105, rue Vercingétorix

Métro line 13, Pernety Station or Plaisance Station

Telephone: 01-45-43-09-84

Open daily, except Sunday, from 7:30 A.M. to 8:00 P.M.

We were interested to learn that this reputable bakery
was once a music store. M. Kamir has had a most
unusual career. He was once a writer for the French news
magazine *Actuel*, and then he operated a music store at
this location, selling Virgin records. In keeping with the
history of the shop, for a while he also sold bread baked
by Lionel Poilâne. When he was advised by the City of
Paris that the building would be demolished, as the
neighborhood was cleared for apartments and other construction, M. Kamir responded quickly. He hired a qualified boulanger and converted the shop to the
distinguished bakery it once was (and is today), thereby
qualifying it for the register of historic buildings and
avoiding demolition. Working and studying along with
the boulanger, he gradually mastered not only the skills
of bread making but the long, hard hours and challenge
of his new occupation. Today he is considered one of the
top bakers of Paris. Even if they run out of bread, this
charming old bakery with a white tile front is worth the
trip. The shop interior has a beautiful ceiling and side
walls of etched glass. Down a narrow staircase to the
basement you will find a fascinating centuries-old wood-

fired oven producing prize-winning bread six days a
week. The **pain biologique,** an organic health loaf, is
their feature, but they make many other varieties of
bread, some sold by the piece or slice. They also have
tartes aux pommes (apple pies), quiches, and pizza.
Boulanger Basil Kamir and Mme. Kamir also have bakeries at the following locations:

> 82, rue Daguerre, in "the Fourteenth"
>
> 166, ave. de Suffren, in "the Fifteenth"
>
> 35, rue Violet, in "the Fifteenth"

Le Moulin de la Vierge

82, rue Daguerre
Métro line 4 or 6, Denfert-Rochereau Station (also R.E.R., B line)
Telephone: 01-43-22-50-55
Open daily, except Sunday, from 7:30 A.M. to 8:00 P.M.

We are told that the four boulangeries of M. and Mme.
Kamir are named for an ancient mill in the Aveyron
region of south central France. You will locate this corner bakery by the side panels, paintings under glass of
nineteenth-century ladies with a shock of wheat. Inside
there are several quaint and fascinating artifacts—old
lamps, scales, and implements. All of the Kamirs' shops
sell their special farine (flour) packed in bags small
enough to take home. The **pain biologique** comes in several sizes, some, such as the **petit pain,** small enough for
snacking on as you walk down the street. There are also

madeleines, coco miel, a confection of honey and coconut, and much more.

LA RONDE DES PAINS

93, rue Raymond-Losserand
Métro line 13, Pernety Station
Autobus route 28 or 62
Telephone: 01-45-42-23-98
Open daily, except Wednesday, from 6:30 A.M. to 8:30 P.M.

You cannot miss this interesting boulangerie with a red-framed duet of puppets in its front window, and as you step inside, you will be greeted by some unusual—and tempting—breads. We liked their **baguette à l'ancienne, baguette paysanne, pain aux six céréales, pain suisse au chorizo et au gruyère,** a bread with sausage and cheese, and the **pain aux noix et aux raisins.** They also feature tarts, éclairs, charlottes, and sandwiches.

ROTTIER BOULANGERIE

24, rue Daguerre
Métro line 4 or 6, Denfert-Rochereau Station (also on the R.E.R.,
    B line)
Telephone: 01-43-22-31-61
Open daily, except Sunday and Monday, from 7:00 A.M. to 8:30 P.M.

At the corner of rue Daguerre, a pedestrian street, and rue Boulard, you will find Rottier. It's two short blocks from **Les Catacombes,** a network of old limestone quarries with piles of bones from Paris's graveyards (it's open only two hours in the afternoon, 2:00 to 4:00 P.M.). This is a very modern bakery, with the exception of the charming glass side panels of windmills on either side of the door and a red tile floor inside. It is also very busy. The boulanger is especially proud of his **tarte aux pommes,** an apple pie. He also features **éclairs** and **sablés.** While the bread varieties are standard, they are of the highest quality.

Arrondissement

*I*t has been said that the most distinctive thing about "the Fifteenth" is its lack of distinction, which can also be interpreted that here you find the genuine Paris, a solid residential neighborhood built a century ago. Across the Seine from the affluence of "the Sixteenth," there are few tour buses and many poodles. In this arrondissement, you are in the shadow of the Eiffel Tower, which is actually in "the Seventh," though quite visible from many vantage points. This arrondissement, however, also has its own tower, the Tour Montparnasse which is 210 meters high compared to the Eiffel Tower's 320 meters. Built by an American company in 1973, the steel monstrosity has never been accepted by Parisians, nor qualified to belong to this venerable section of the city. The Métro is elevated on boulevard de Grenelle, and below the Dupleix Station, there is a street market under the Métro tracks, extending east to rue du Commerce. This market has everything to offer, and many bargains, but by 5:00 P.M., it is swept clean—so plan to shop early. The market is held on Wednesday and Sunday. L'Institut Pasteur and the Musée de la Poste are attractions close to the Tour Montparnasse. "The Fifteenth" has many authentic bakeries. We have selected the following for your exploration and enjoyment.

ℬoulangerie ℬourlier

54, rue du Commerce

Métro line 8, Commerce Station, or Métro line 10, Émile Zola Station

Telephone: 01-45-79-78-07

Open daily, except Monday, from 7:30 A.M. to 9:00 P.M.

One's attention is attracted to this small, yet very busy, neighborhood bakery by a huge pottery pitcher with flowers in the window. They also display the familiar blue sign of the authentic boulanger. **Pain de campagne** is featured, but there are many additional delicacies: **flan à l'abricot** (apricot flan), **macarons**, **croque-monsieur**, quiches, pizza, and other interesting choices.

𝒞haillou, 𝒥ean-Pierre

25, rue de Lourmel

Métro line 6, Dupleix Station

Autobus route 42

Telephone: 01-45-78-93-16

Open daily, except Thursday and Friday, from 7:00 A.M. to 8:00 P.M.

It was lunch time when we visited M. Chaillou's bakery, so there was no way to resist his toasted **croque-**

monsieur, and though we had enjoyed others, his rated close to ten on a scale of one to ten. Dozens of special breads are featured in this bakery, including **pain de campagne, pain de seigle aux raisins, petits pains, croissants,** and **baguettes.** On the top of the list is his signature pastry, the **tarte normande.**

Delmas, Jean Claude

93, rue du Commerce

Métro line 8, Commerce Station or Felix Fauré Station

Autobus route 70

Telephone: 01-48-28-65-86

Open daily, except Monday, from 7:00 A.M. to 8:30 P.M.

M. Delmas takes great pride in his rustic **boule paysanne** and his **pain au levain.** In all, he makes sixteen varieties of bread. The pastry shelves abound with quiches in small individual sizes and tarts of several varieties. He also makes **tortière,** a specialty pastry dish filled with prunes and flavored with a brandy from southwest France. He also sells sandwiches and pizza.

A̶u F̶in P̶alais

18, rue Valentin Haüy

Métro line 10, Ségur Station, or Métro line 6, Sèvres-Lecourbe
Station

Telephone: 01-43-06-03-61

Open daily, except Wednesday, from 7:00 A.M. to 9:00 P.M.

There is a statue of Louis Pasteur centered in the Place
de Breteuil, a few steps from this boulangerie, and if you
continue north, you will be at the **Église du Dôme**, the
tomb of Napoléon. Au Fin Palais is a small, modern bakery—neat, clean, and bright—in an upscale neighborhood. The boulanger is very friendly and interested in
quality products. The Banette sign is prominent and specialties include **pain au levain** and **pain aux céréales**. The
pastry display is particularly enticing, with tartelettes in
several flavors and delicious tourtes. The **tourte au
saumon** is especially tasty.

GRANGIER, FRANCIS

49, rue Cambronne
Métro line 6, Cambronne Station
Autobus route 49
Telephone: 01-42-73-10-74
Open daily, except Monday, from 7:00 A.M. to 2:00 P.M. and from
3:30 P.M. to 7:30 P.M.

M. and Mme. Grangier showed us several unusual breads
made with Banette flour: **Banette moisson,** a harvest
bread; **pain aux châtaignes** (chestnut bread); **pain à l'ancienne; fougasse garnie,** a crusty latticelike bread of
baguette dough with olives, bacon, and cheese; **brioche;
croissants aux amandes;** and more. For your sweet tooth
there is **kugelhopf,** a crown-shaped, Alsacian yeast cake
with almonds and raisins, and a beautiful cake called
gâteau William. And we will not forget their chocolates,
particularly the **chocolats pompadour.**

LA GRENELLOISE

65, rue des Entrepreneurs
Métro line 10, Charles Michel Station
Autobus route 70
Telephone: 01-45-77-24-87
Open daily, except Monday, from 7:00 A.M. to 8:30 P.M.

A sign at this interesting corner bakery reads: "Les Animaux," announcing their featured breads made in the

shape of animals, **pain de formes différentes et en animaux.** They also make **pain complet, pain de seigle, petits pains,** and **pains de fantaisie,** several imaginatively shaped breads. There are many pastries too, as well as sandwiches, pizza, and quiches.

LEVILLE, GÉRARD

11, Place Charles Michel

Métro line 10, Charles Michel Station

Autobus route 42 or 70

Telephone: 01-45-78-27-82

Open daily, except Monday, from 7:00 A.M. to 8:00 P.M

This bright, cheerful corner bakery has butter croissants for less than five francs ($1.00 US)! They have many varieties of bread, too: **Banette moisson, pain au levain,** and **baguettes** of every length. You will be tempted by their **sablés aux pruneaux et framboises** (prune and raspberry shortbreads), tea cakes shaped like financiers but called madeleines, jams, jellies, and ice cream.

ℒIONEL 𝒫OILÂNE

49, blvd. de Grenelle

Métro line 6, Bir-Hakeim Station or Dupleix Station

Telephone: 01-45-79-11-49

Open daily, except Monday, from 7:15 A.M. to 8:15 P.M.

Some refer to Poilâne on Grenelle as a clone of the original boulangerie on rue du Cherche-Midi, but we found it very much a distinctive boulangerie in its own right. They sell the famous **boules** decorated with bread dough resembling wheat and grapevines. You can buy the boule by the slice or by the four-pound loaf. Most travelers prefer it by the slice. You'll see them munching the bread while walking down the street. The shop gives out cookie samples to satisfy you as you wait your turn at this busy shop. They also sell linen bread bags printed with the famous Poilâne name—great for storing your bread. Lionel Poilâne has another bakery at 8, rue du Cherche-Midi, in "the Sixth."

ℳAISON 𝒮ERGENT

133, ave. Émile Zola

Métro line 10, Émile Zola Station

Telephone: 01-45-75-20-64

Open daily, except Sunday, from 7:00 A.M. to 8:00 P.M.

The awning tells us the pâtissier is M. Jourdan, apparently the previous owner, but now M. Sergent is very much in charge. He displays the familiar red Banette sign, and several breads feature the name—**Banette au levain, complet, de son, rustique, au sésame, de campagne,** and **pain de mie.** He also bakes pastries—**florentines** and **tartes au citron, à la framboise, à la fraise, à la cerise, à la mûre**—and a variety of takeouts like sandwiches, salads, pizza, and cold soda.

Max Poilâne

87, rue Brancion

Métro line 13, Porte de Vanves Station

Telephone. 01-48-28-45-90

Open daily, except Sunday, from 7:15 A.M. to 8:00 P.M.

Yes, there are two Poilânes, and while Lionel may have profited from more publicity, brother Max is also an artisan and a well-known boulanger with a commanding line of very high quality bread. His large, round country loaf made with natural leaven and stone-ground brown flour is his signature bread. He also bakes a wonderful rye bread and **pains de méteil** (whole-wheat rolls). The shop has sparkling marble floors, decorated mirrors, and a glistening chandelier, and his wood-fired ovens operate around the clock, producing delicious, wonderful bread. Max Poilâne does not make a baguette, but he does make **pain de mie,** a square-loafed white bread with virtually no crust. Don't forget dessert, because his **bouchons** (chocolate cupcakes) are irresistible. Max Poilâne has two other locations. He spends most of his time baking here at the rue Brancion location, but all three are rewarding destinations as you explore Paris's finest bakeries.

His other two locations: 42, Place du Marché St. Honoré, in "the First," and 29, rue de l'Ouest, in "the Fourteenth."

MICHEL JOUBERT

33, blvd. de Grenelle

Métro line 6, Dupleix Station

Autobus route 42

Telephone: 01-45-78-10-32

Open daily, except Tuesday, from 6:45 A.M. to 8:00 P.M.

We always ask the question "Faites-vous le pain vous même?" M. Joubert underlined his resounding "Oui." Indeed, his many breads are baked right in his boulangerie. In this bakery you'll find odd-shaped **pain de fantaisie, baguette épi, pain diététique sans sel** (salt-free diet bread), and display cases of pastries and sandwiches that will tempt you to return for lunch. They also feature open-faced croissants with grated cheese, **tartelettes aux épinards** (spinach tarts), hot dogs with cheese, homemade jams, honey caramels, and chocolate truffles.

Micheline Mareau

22, rue Cambronne

Métro line 6, Cambronne Station

Autobus route 49 or 80

Telephone: 01-43-06-04-28

Open daily, except Sunday, from 6:30 A.M. to 8:00 P.M.

We like a shop that has candy for children, so they can put a single franc on the counter and receive smiles and candy in return—though in Paris, the children sometimes prefer a small baguette or pastry. This attractive bakery has something for everyone—**baguettes à l'ancienne** (old-fashioned baguettes), **pain de seigle au pavot** (rye bread with poppy seeds), **pain de campagne en tranche** (sliced country-style bread), **fougasses aux lardons et gruyère** (fougasses with bacon and gruyère cheese), panini sandwiches, **petites galettes** (small cookies), chocolates, and meringues.

ℒE ℳOULIN DE LA ℣IERGE

166, ave. de Suffren

Métro line 6, Sèvres-Lecourbe Station or Cambronne Station, or

   Métro line 10, Ségur Station

Telephone: 01-47-83-45-55

Open daily, except Sunday, from 7:00 A.M. to 8:00 P.M.

This boulangerie, close to the **Tour Eiffel** and the **École Militaire,** is the largest of Basil Kamir's four boulangeries. We refer you to the story of M. Kamir's career in the listing of his bakery in "the Fourteenth." This is a charming bakery, with an attractive lamp in the window, an unusual tile floor, and many antiques. A delightful bakery scene with miniature, mechanized bakers—one kneading dough, the other bringing bread from the small brick oven—is in one of the windows, certain to charm children and adults alike. Inside you will find one of Paris's most complete displays of breads: **pain biologique au levain** (leavened organic bread); **pain complet; pain grenobles** (a special nut and raisin bread); and **fougasse,** his with olives and anchovies. He also sells many pastries, including **tartes aux pommes, au citron, et aux framboises** (apple, lemon, and raspberry pies). This is a bakery well worth a stop!

LE MOULIN DE LA VIERGE

35, rue Violet

Métro line 6, Dupleix Station

Telephone: 01-45-75-85-85

Open daily, except Saturday and Sunday, from 7:30 A.M. to 8:00 P.M.

This bakery is perhaps a bit less quaint than M. Kamir's other three boulangeries. We still recommend this corner bakery on rue Violet, close to the elevated Métro on busy boulevard de Grenelle, as a destination. The wonderful breads and pastries, all baked on the premises by one of the top bakers in Paris and his staff, feature the same quality products of this famous boulanger.

PHILLIPPE THILLOUX

24, rue du Commerce

Métro line 6 or Métro line 10, La Motte-Picquet-Grenelle Station

Telephone: 01-45-75-11-62

Open daily, except Sunday, from 7:00 A.M. to 9:00 P.M.

Although this shop has no shortage of bread, the special attraction is its **confiserie** (confectionery), with endless trays of irresistible desserts, as well as sandwiches, quiches, salads, and chocolates. You can enjoy a delicious ham and Brie sandwich, or whatever else appeals to you from the many selections, at a small area in the shop with tables and chairs.

℘ICHARD

88, rue de Cambronne

Métro line 12, Vaugirard Station

Autobus route 89, 29, 70, or 69

Telephone: 01-43-06-97-37

Open daily, except Monday and Tuesday, from 7:00 A.M. to
    1:30 P.M. and from 4:00 P.M. to 8:00 P.M.

M. Pichard is a very friendly artisan boulanger, whose products have been awarded high honors. Some of his specialties include **le forrestier au seigle et céréales** (forest rye bread), **pain complet aux noix et noisettes** (whole-wheat bread with walnuts and hazelnuts), **pain de tradition française, pain bâtard, nature-vie** (wholly natural bread), **l'intégral, la baguette Pichard, le Sully pâtisserie, la bombe Joséphine,** and **la tourte trianon.** Pichard's is also an upscale eating establishment, offering salads, quiches, croissant sandwiches, fruit tarts, chocolates, and various pastries.

ARRONDISSEMENT

*I*f we dare make a comparison, "the Sixteenth" is to Parisians what Park Avenue is to New Yorkers— high fashioned, sophisticated, glamorous, and upscale.

The Boulevard Périphérique, Paris's circumferential highway, and the Bois de Boulogne border the arrondissement on the west; on the east, it is bordered by the Seine. The Place Charles de Gaulle-Étoile and the Arc de Triomphe clearly define the northern boundary, and "the Sixteenth" extends far south, to Porte de St. Cloud.

The creation of the arrondissement is recent history, dating to 1860, when three villages—Auteuil, Passy, and Chaillot—merged and joined Paris. There are many attractions in this district: well-manicured parks, stately boulevards leading to the Arc de Triomphe, the Jardins du Trocadéro, the Palais de Chaillot, sixty-four foreign embassies, and the Musée du Vin (the Paris wine museum). Much of the city's reconstruction from the mid-nineteenth century is found in "the Sixteenth," with perhaps the best example being avenue Foch, one of Paris's grandest boulevards. The beauty, dignity, and opulence of this arrondissement are hard to deny.

ÉCHU

118, ave. Victor Hugo

Métro line 2, Victor Hugo Station, or Métro line 9, Rue de la Pompe
Station

Telephone: 01-47-27-97-79

Open daily, except Monday, from 7:00 A.M. to 8:00 P.M.

You cannot miss this corner bakery on the fashionable avenue Victor Hugo. They pride themselves on **la vrai baguette française** (the genuine French baguette), **croissants aux amandes, tartes au citron, petits pains au chocolat** (chocolate rolls), and a hearty **pain rustique.** The **mousse au chocolat** is hard to turn down.

BOULANGERIE S.A. DESGRANGES

6, rue de Passy

Métro line 6, Passy Station

Autobus route 32 or 52

Telephone: 01-42-88-35-82

Open daily, except Tuesday, from 7:00 A.M. to 8:00 P.M.

The **Tour Eiffel** is visible across the Seine from the neighborhood served by the Passy Métro station, and the **Jardins du Trocadéro** are just a short walk north of this boulangerie, a contemporary bakery where there is adequate bread but where the thrust is also pastry and takeouts. One specialty is **pain décoré,** bread decorated to order with family and fraternal insignia. Our visit here was late in the afternoon, so the bread selection was somewhat sparce, actually a good sign, because the local customers never stopped coming in the door. We also saw tempting pastries—**opéras, tartes, gâteaux, petits fours**—and they offer quite a menu of pizza, salads, quiches, lasagna, and more for takeout.

CARTON

150, ave. Victor Hugo

Métro line 2, Victor Hugo Station, or Métro line 9, rue de la Pompe
  Station

Autobus route 52

Telephone: 01-47-04-66-55

Open daily, except Monday, from 7:00 A.M. to 8:00 P.M.

M. and Mme. Jean Pierre Carton operate this elegant
bakery near many attractions: the Place Victor Hugo,
avenue Foch, the **Trocadéro,** and the **Bois de Boulogne.**
They list several special breads: **pain de campagne
au levain, pain de seigle aux raisins et aux noix,
baguette au fromage** (cheese baguette), **pain biologique**
("lemaire"). This boulangerie is also a great stop for
lunch; they have lovely sandwiches and salads, wine, cold
drinks, and coffee.

DÉLICES D'AUTEUIL

78, rue Michel-Ange

Métro line 9, Exelmans Station

Telephone: 01-46-51-08-64

Open daily, except Sunday, from 7:00 A.M. to 8:00 P.M.

Located in the south quarter of "the Sixteenth," three
blocks west of the **Parc des Princes** and the **Stade Jean
Rouin,** a major sports arena, M. Gautier displays very
attractive breads of every description and an ample

choice of pastries. He features **pain à l'ancienne** (old-style bread).

À LA FLÛTE ENCHANTÉE

7, ave. Mozart

Métro line 6, Passy Station, or Métro line 9, La Muette Station

Telephone: 01-45-27-05-92

Open daily, except Sunday, from 6:00 A.M. to 8:00 P.M.

Located a short distance from the **Jardin du Ranelagh,** one of many small parks in "the Sixteenth," this charming bakery offers a chance for a modest picnic. They have a tempting line of breads, featuring traditional **baguettes,** a **délice aux noix,** a walnut delicacy, and **le Mozart,** a special pastry.

À LA FLÛTE ENCHANTÉE

46, rue de Passy

Métro line 6, Passy Station

Telephone: 01-42-88-51-27

Open daily, except Sunday, from 6:45 A.M. to 8:00 P.M.

This is the second boulangerie bearing the name À la Flûte Enchantée (the magic flute), which refers to Mozart but is also a reference to the **flûte,** the slender roll that we have seen in other bakeries. As you ascend to the bakery from the Passy Métro station, you are close to the

Musée du Vin—the Paris wine museum. The bakery has counters inside where you can enjoy the selection of tempting snacks and breads. The traditional line of breads is wonderful, and it is matched in quality by the confections and pastries: **financiers, tartes aux pommes** (apple pies), and more. There is also a crêpe machine pushed out on the sidewalk. Even the light rain does not discourage customers from lining up ouside for their crêpes.

LA FONTAINE D'AUTEUIL

26, rue de la Tour

Métro line 6, Trocadéro Station or Passy Station, or Métro line 9, Trocadéro Station

Autobus route 22 or 32

Telephone: 01-45-20-58-72

Open daily, except Sunday, from 7:00 A.M. to 8:00 P.M.

The **Eiffel Tower** is clearly visible across the Seine from the rue de la Tour, hence its name. The manager and the owner of La Fontaine d'Auteuil, both charming, intelligent women, are interested in quality bakery products and natural ingredients. This most interesting neighborhood bakery is operated by the master boulanger A. D. Lamourdedieu. His **pain de seigle au son complet** is a superb loaf, and his **pain naturel biologique,** a small, round bread made from natural biological flour, is crusty on the outside, with a honey-colored interior that is moist and chewy. Also listed as specialties are his mouth-watering chocolate and orange puddings. M. Lamourdedieu creates lovely decorated pastries and also designs orders for special occasions.

LA GRIGNOTIÈRE

84, rue Lauriston

Métro line 6, Trocadéro Station or Boissière Station, or Métro line 9, Trocadéro Station

Telephone: 01-47-27-90-21

Open daily, except Saturday and Sunday, from 7:00 A.M. to 8:00 P.M.

Jean Antract is the artisan boulanger at this fascinating shop with an interesting name, derived from the phrase *grigne du pain* (the network of fibers where a loaf is cut) and the word *grignoter* (to nibble at food). This shop is close to area parks where you can enjoy the special breads, including a great sourdough, chocolate tarts, macaroons, and an irresistible **gâteau au chocolat.**

Joël Roy

34, ave. de Versailles

Métro line 10, Mirabeau Station

Autobus route 72

Telephone: 01-42-88-59-13

Open daily, except Monday, from 7:00 A.M. to 8:30 P.M.

This interesting bake shop is a short walk south from the largest building in France, the **Maison de Radio France,** headquarters of the French national radio. They have a complete line of wonderful breads, yet list as their specialties several tempting desserts: **royal chocolat délicieux** (a chocolate cake), **meringues, nougats,** and much more.

Michel Geffroy

77, ave. Kleber

Métro line 6, Boissière Station, or Métro line 9, Trocadéro Station

Autobus route 30 or 22

Telephone: 01-47-27-92-79

Open daily, except Saturday, from 6:30 A.M. to 8:00 P.M.

Avenue Kleber is one of Paris's fashionable thoroughfares, one of the spokes leading to the **Place Charles de Gaulle.** We expected to find attractive bakeries in this area, and we were not disappointed. M. Geffroy has a full line of breads, in addition to pastries and chocolates. His business card reads: "Qualité d'Abord" (quality first). You will be delighted with this establishment.

ℳocquery

163, ave. de Versailles

Métro line 9, Exelmans Station

Autobus route 22 or 72

Telephone: 01-42-88-72-12

Open daily, except Sunday, from 7:15 A.M. to 8:30 P.M.

In the south quarter of the arrondissement you will find this prototype of the neighborhood bakery, with a steady stream of customers—people buying half of a baguette, others studying the pastry case to make their selection. With an abundant inventory of attractive breads as well as sandwiches, cold salads, and warm dishes, we found it difficult to list any one specialty. M. Mocquery, artisan baker, does it right.

ℛayer

186, ave. de Versailles

Métro line 9, Porte de St. Cloud Station

Autobus route 72 or 62

Telephone: 01-45-25-41-33

Open daily, except Tuesday and Wednesday, from 7:00 A.M. to
   8:00 P.M.

The southernmost quarter of "the Sixteenth," the Auteuil, is a bit removed from the high fashion of the northern sections, yet close to many parks, recreation areas, and sports arenas. M. Rayer offers everything you need for a delightful picnic and has a complete inventory of the popular breads, croissants, and pastries as well.

Roulleau

33, rue Lauriston

Métro line 6, Kleber Station or Charles de Gaulle-Étoile Station, or

Métro line 1 or 2, Charles de Gaulle-Étoile Station

Telephone: 01-47-27-63-20

Open daily from 7:00 A.M. to 8:00 P.M.

Special breads at this fashionable stop include **pain complet** and **pain de seigle au son et céréales.** There are also pastries, salads, and sandwiches to enjoy at the tables inside, or to take along with you. Here you are within walking distance to the **Arc de Triomphe.**

𝒱AUTIER

152, ave. de Versailles

Métro line 9, Exelmans Station

Autobus route 22 or 72

Telephone: 01-42-24-45-32

Open daily, except Tuesday, from 7:00 A.M. to 8:00 P.M.

Artisan baker J. Vautier operates this friendly, very attractive bakery in the south quarter of the arrondissement, just a block from the Seine and quite close to the **Bois de Boulogne** when you walk in the other direction. In this area you will find a number of parks, the largest concentration in Paris, with something of interest for everyone. The shop offers great variety too. We liked the **croissant au chocolat,** the **pain brioché aux raisins,** and the **pain de son** (bran bread). The window display of pâtisseries is varied and elegant.

ARRONDISSEMENT

$\mathcal{T}$hose who write travel books find it difficult to credit "the Seventeenth" with any must-see attraction. Some might claim the Arc de Triomphe, in the southwest corner, but "the Eighth" and "the Sixteenth" also have just claim to that monument. A few blocks west on the avenue de la Grande Armée is the Place de la Porte Maillot, important to tourists as the terminal for the Air France bus to Aéroport Charles de Gaulle. This section of the arrondissement is an upscale neighborhood of obvious bourgeois respectability, but as one advances to the north and east sections, changes in lifestyle and general maintenance are evident. "The Seventeenth" can best be described as a heavily populated section of Paris offering interesting contrast between the several neighborhoods. To the bakery explorer, this means a great choice from the many boulangeries undisturbed by tour buses. You will meet some friendly, helpful shopkeepers, and often the patron himself or herself, as you visit the recommended bakeries. A subtle purpose of this directory is to encourage the visitor to Paris to abandon, at times, the frequently identified attractions in every tour guide in favor of a venture into the residential neighborhoods. "The Seventeenth" thereby qualifies!

Aux Armes de Niel

29, ave. Niel

Métro line 2, Ternes Station

Autobus route 30

Telephone: 01-47-63-62-01

Open weekdays, except Tuesday, from 6:30 A.M. to 8:30 P.M.

Open Saturday from 7:00 A.M. to 8:30 P.M.

Open Sunday from 7:00 A.M. to 1:30 P.M. and from 2:00 P.M. to 8:30 P.M.

This bakery specializes in decorative bread for special occasions—huge, round, and beautiful breads, but not made for sampling. They also feature a sourdough baguette, ficelle au levain, and packets of biscotti, a tasty Italian biscuit often eaten at breakfast. Avenue Niel continues south as avenue Mac-Mahon, converging on the Charles de Gaulle-Étoile, so this bakery is quite close to the center of Paris tourism.

ℬEAUCOURT

55, blvd. Gouvion Saint Cyr

Métro line 1, Porte Maillot Station

Autobus route 43

Telephone: 01-45-74-04-50

Open daily, except Wednesday, from 7:00 A.M. to 9:00 P.M.

As you leave the Porte Maillot Métro station, you pass the terminal for the Air France buses to **Aéroport Charles de Gaulle,** the huge **Palais des Congrès,** major hotels—the **Concorde Lafayette** and the **Méridien**—and then come to this small, friendly neighborhood boulangerie displaying the coveted blue sign of the artisan baker. Their special breads are leavened, and though it was late in the day and the shelves had served many customers, we still could sample the excellent products.

ℬOULANGERIE D'ANTAN

6, rue de Levis

Métro line 2 or 3, Villiers Station

Autobus route 30

Telephone: 01-43-87-26-35

Open daily, except Wednesday, from 7:00 A.M. to 8:30 P.M.

Antan means "yesteryear," so one can expect old-fashioned breads as featured products at this boulangerie. There is another boulangerie with a similar name in "the Eighteenth," but it is not related to this bakery in any way. **Pain de campagne** is prominent in this bakery. They also make **pain viennois,** a step up from the more common baguette. From the pastry display, we picked their **mille-feuille,** absolutely irresistible. Be sure to try the **noix de coco banane** (coconut with nuts and bananas) and the exquisite **macarons** and **éclairs.** These folks make their own chocolate too.

BOULANGERIE BIGOT

11, rue Gustave Flaubert

Métro line 2, Ternes Station

Autobus route 30

Telephone: 01 47-63-75-68

Open daily, except Sunday, from 7:00 A.M. to 8:00 P.M.

On the corner of rue Rennequin and rue Gustave Flaubert, one block removed from the heavy traffic on avenue de Wagram, you will find this gleaming white bakery with a gold-lettered sign, the boulangerie of M. and Mme. François Bigot. The **Parc Monceau,** a favorite picnic location in "the Seventeenth," is a brisk walk away. F. Bigot displays the Retrodor sign, assuring customers of the consistent quality of his flour. Featured breads include **pain rustique au levain naturel,** a naturally leavened rustic, hearty loaf, and the **baguette Retrodor,** a special baguette from a Retrodor recipe. They also have many varieties of tarts, quiches, small pizzas, baguette sandwiches, and their own chocolates (somehow chocolates are always better when made in the patron's kitchen).

CLEMENT, NOËL

120, ave. de Villiers

Métro line 3, Péreire Station or Porte de Champerret Station

Autobus route 84, 92, or 93

Telephone: 01-47-63-40-90

Open daily, except Wednesday, from 7:15 A.M. to 8:00 P.M.

M. Clement's highly recommended boulangerie is in an upscale section of "the Seventeenth." One's first impression of the bakery is the window on the corner with large shocks of wheat and porcelain figures of a baker and his lady—a most attractive display. You will not be disappointed once inside. The baguettes, croissants, and raisin bread are all outstanding. The **feuilletés** (flaky puff pastries) are among the finest we have seen, as are his **mini ficelles.** The sandwich selections, salads, chocolates, jams, and quiches are numerous and tempting.

ℭOUASNON

21, rue de Levis

Métro line 2 or 3, Villiers Station

Telephone: 01-43-87-28-27

Open daily, except Monday, from 7:00 A.M. to 8:45 P.M.

The boulanger's specialty, **pain paillasse,** a stone-shaped country loaf, is displayed in the window of this small, very attractive bakery on a pedestrian street near a Monoprix. Inside you can see the bakers hard at work from the sales area, an added attraction. Tiles on the floor of the bakery spell out "Artisan Boulanger." The **pain souverain** (bread of the highest quality) is the boulanger's special pride. You will also like his pastries, especially the **biscuits à four sec, éclairs, macarons,** and his great quantity of attractive and tasty **tartelettes.**

ℒES 𝒟ÉLICES DE ℳONCEAU

153, blvd. Malesherbes

Métro line 3, Malesherbes Station or Wagram Station

Telephone: 01-42-27-86-02

Open daily, except Sunday, from 7:30 A.M. to 8:00 P.M.

M. Jean-Claude Roulleau operates this small corner bakery on boulevard Malesherbes, at Place de Nicaragua, not far from Place du Général Catroux, a small park perfect for a picnic with the tempting inventory of takeout foods at the bakery. While we observed a variety of breads, the sandwiches, warm and cold plates, and numerous pastries really caught our attention.

D. FILLOUX

12, ave. Mac-Mahon

Métro line 1, 6, or 2, Charles de Gaulle-Étoile Station

Autobus route 92

Telephone: 01-43-80-06-04

Open daily from 7:00 A.M. to 8:00 P.M.

The **Arc de Triomphe** is clearly in view from M. Filloux's boulangerie on the picturesque avenue Mac-Mahon, one of many broad avenues converging on the Charles de Gaulle-Étoile. His **bûcheron,** a rugged whole-wheat loaf, and his **pain aux sept céréales** are most interesting. A sign on his window assured us that breads were baked on the premises: "Pains fabrication maison cuits sur place." His pastries, quiches, flans, and sandwiches are also very attractive.

GOUDENHOOFT, GUY

59, ave. des Ternes

Métro line 2, Ternes Station, or Métro line 1, 2, or 6, Charles de
    Gaulle-Étoile Station

Telephone: 01-45-74-27-14

Open daily, except Wednesday, from 7:00 A.M. to 8:00 P.M.

The avenue des Ternes, continuing parallel to the avenue des Champs-Élysées as rue du Faubourg St.-Honoré, is one of Paris's most fashionable streets. The Arc de Triomphe is a short walk south. We were attracted to M. Goudenhooft's bakery by a unique artistically decorated pastry cover for a bottle of Beaujolais, in season at the time. He also features several unusual breads: **pain faluche** (soda bread), **pain en animaux** (breads shaped like animals), and **Banette au levain naturel.** It was time for a mid-morning snack when we were there, and his danois et café (danish and coffee) filled the bill. The Dutch heritage of the patron is evident in many of his fine products.

JOUSSET, RENÉ

38, rue des Batignolles

Métro line 2, Rome Station

Autobus route 66

Telephone: 01-45-22 45-04

Open daily, except Sunday, from 6:45 A.M. to 8:00 P.M.

M. Jousset's attractive boulangerie is in the southeast corner of the arrondissement, not far from the town hall. He features several country-style breads: **pain paysan, baguette de campagne,** and **pain de campagne.** We also liked his **pain aux noix** (walnut bread) and **fougasse,** a special twisted dough with herbs and garnish. He has a beautiful **gâteau au chocolat** (chocolate cake) and a **gâteau de la maison,** which is a special fruitcake, as well as tarts offered in a wide choice of flavors. On his takeout counter, we found sandwiches and small pizzas, no larger than six inches—all ready to go.

Jouvin, Michel

19, ave. des Ternes

Métro line 2, Ternes Station

Autobus route 30

Telephone: 01-43-80-23-28

Open daily, except Sunday, from 7:30 A.M. to 8:00 P.M.

This small bakery with the red Banette sign is apparently the favorite luncheon choice of local police, who lined up three abreast to order quiche, pizza, "hot dogs," and **baguettes au jambon et fromage.** They also feature a **chausson,** a luncheon item similar to a turnover. They make at least twenty varieties of bread, including a very attractive **brioche; pain sologne,** a special recipe from the Sologne region; and **pain de sol,** an earthy, authentic cereal bread. This bakery is quite close to the **Arc de Triomphe** and the busiest thoroughfare in all Paris—the **Champs-Élysées.**

LEMONNIER FRÈRES

100, ave. Niel

Métro line 3, Péreire Station

Autobus route 92 or 93

Telephone: 01-43-80-03-32

Open daily, except Sunday, from 6:30 A.M. to 8:00 P.M.

We were advised of a pending change in the management of this busy bakery on avenue Niel, yet assured that the high quality of the products will continue. Indeed, we sampled traditional breads, a **croissant aux amandes, crêpes,** and **tartes au citron, à la fraise, aux pommes** and **au kiwi.** They also sell **panini** and other sandwiches.

MARINIER, PASCAL

100, rue des Dames

Métro line 2 or 3, Villiers Station, or Métro line 2, Rome Station

Telephone: 01-43-87-25-37

Open daily, except Thursday, from 7:00 A.M. to 8:30 or 9:00 P.M.

In the southeast corner of "the Seventeenth," a short distance from the **mairie** (town hall), near where the rue des Dames crosses the tracks north from **Gare St. Lazare,** you will find this small, very neat, and clean boulangerie. To further identify the shop, look for a stuffed duck and fresh flowers in the window. Inside, the shop has a decorated alabaster ceiling. M. Marinier's specialties include **pain au levain naturel, pain aux pommes** (apple bread),

baguette de tradition française, and **tartelette au citron à l'ancienne,** an old-fashioned lemon pastry that makes a choice midmorning snack.

ℳEUNIER

140, ave. de Clichy

Métro line 13, Brochant Station

Autobus route 74, 54, or 31

Telephone: 01-46-27-07-33

Open daily, except Tuesday, from 6:30 A.M. to 9:00 P.M.

This small boulangerie proudly displays the familiar blue sign designating an artisan boulanger as the patron, specializing in breads, pastries, and delicatessen items. There is a famous market, the **Marché des Batignolles,** and an attractive park, the **Square des Batignolles,** within easy walking distance. We liked his **recette du pain suisse redécouverte pour vous,** Swiss bread from a rediscovered recipe; **baguette au le-vain; baguette aux céréales;** and **pain de campagne aux noix et gruyère,** a country-style bread with nuts and gruyère cheese.

Mic Mac

99, ave. de Clichy

Métro line 13, Brochant Station or La Fourche Station

Autobus route 74

Telephone: 01-42-63-61-59

Open daily from 6:00 A.M. to 11:00 P.M.

This bakery is practically a round the-clock operation—open every day for seventeen hours! It offers special breads and pastry delicacies quite different from those in most Paris bakeries. Recipes from Tunis, Turkey, and Morocco prevail. For variety and some pleasing taste sensations, stop by Mic Mac.

Overghemi

87, ave. de Clichy

Métro line 13, Porte de Clichy Station or Brochant Station

Autobus route 54 or 74

Telephone: 01-42-26-07-46

Open daily, except Wednesday, from 7:00 A.M. to 8:00 P.M.

The very busy Place de Clichy bakery is one block down the avenue from, and an equal distance east of, one of Paris's most famous cemeteries, the **Cimetière de Montmartre,** where you will be directed to the graves of Alexandre Dumas, Jacques Offenbach, and other notables. This small corner bakery has a complete line of breads: **pain complet, pain de seigle,** and **pain de**

campagne. It also features several quiches—**quiche aux légumes** (vegetable quiche), **quiche au fromage** (cheese quiche), and **quiche à la saucisse** (sausage quiche)—as well as a variety of sandwiches and pizza.

 PANILEX

176, ave. de Clichy

Métro line 13, Porte de Clichy Station or Brochant Station

Autobus route 54 or 74

Telephone: 01-46-27-80-85

Open daily from 7:00 A.M. to 8:00 P.M.

An extensive industrial area—the **Batignolles**—and the railway tracks to **Gare St. Lazare** border these blocks on avenue de Clichy, yet here we found a large, attractive boulangerie with the blue artisan boulanger decal on the window, a bakery open seven days a week, thirteen hours a day. The listed bread and pastry specialties are français and européens. It is fun and pleasing to sample the breads and delicacies with a German, Dutch, or Scandinavian flair. You will recognize this bakery by the interesting decorative tile on the front panel.

SCHAEFER

20, blvd. des Batignolles

Métro line 2 or 13, Place de Clichy Station

Autobus route 30

Telephone: 01-42-93-15-03

Open daily, except Monday, from 7:30 A.M. to 8:00 P.M.

M. Schaefer's boulangerie is on the corner of rue Darcet and the busy thoroughfare boulevard des Batignolles, just two blocks from the **Place de Clichy.** The town hall for "the Seventeenth" is three blocks west. The selection of bread at this bakery was limited, because our visit was late in the day, but we were assured that all traditional breads are available. We were impressed by some beautiful pastries, especially the **tartelette à l'abricot** (apricot tart), **tartelette aux poires** (pear tart), and **tartelette à la crème** (custard-filled tart). You can watch part of the baking operation from the front of the shop—always an interesting feature.

S.N.C. DES TERNES

91, ave. des Ternes
Métro line 1, Porte Maillot Station
Autobus route 43
Telephone: 01-45-74-10-48
Open daily, except Sunday, from 6:30 A.M. to 9:00 P.M.

This bakery is in the southwest section of "the Seventeenth," not far from the Place de la Porte Maillot and two large hotels—the **Concorde Lafayette** and the **Méridien.** M. and Mme. Gaborit list several bread specialties: **pain au sésame, pain de campagne, pain complet, pain de son, pain de seigle,** and **pain aux céréales.** There are tables inside for coffee and snacks—sandwiches, quiches, and chocolates.

TAILPIED, SERGE

31, rue des Batignolles
Métro line 2, Rome Station
Autobus route 66
Telephone: 01-43-87-78-53
Open daily, except Wednesday, from 7:00 A.M. to 8:30 P.M.

This boulangerie is very close to the town hall. Of special interest is the decorated interior of the shop, a delightful wall of tiles featuring a girl with blonde pigtails and a basket of delicacies. The bread display offers **pain de campagne** and baguettes of several sizes. We liked the meringues—some shaped like a basket for filling with one's favorite fruit or custard—and their chocolate and lemon tarts. They also make a wonderful **quiche aux épinards** (spinach quiche) and our favorite, **quiche au fromage** (cheese quiche).

ARRONDISSEMENT

*Y*ou may use a Métro ticket on the funicular or ascend Montmartre via the cobblestone stairs on rue Foyatier or choose a more gradual climb from east of the Sacré-Coeur, but one way or another, the visitor to Paris is attracted to the "Hill of the Martyrs." By all measures of elevation Paris is quite flat, so any hill is an attraction, and Montmartre, with history dating from A.D. 272, narrow medieval streets, charming shops, and famous churches, is on every tour bus itinerary. The Basilique du Sacré-Coeur, gleaming white, is seen from the sprawling city below. Less noticeable is the very old Église St. Pierre, built in 1134, snuggling up to the twentieth-century edifice. "The Eighteenth" is bordered on the east by the tracks extending from the Gare du Nord and on the north by the Porte de Clignancourt, site of Europe's biggest flea market. The south border is boulevard de Clichy, with less reputable destinations from Pigalle and Anvers Métro stations. The legendary Moulin Rouge is there, famous in film and fiction. There is a working moulin (windmill) in the west section of the arrondissement, where farms and vineyards were cultivated until recent years. And this interesting arrondissement has a cemetery; in the west section, not far from the windmill, is the Cimetière de Montmartre, where many notables are buried. For those seeking a market, try a picturesque one on rue du Poteau, above the Sacré-Coeur, or the crowded street of fabrics, rue Steinkerque, leading to the Anvers Métro station. "The Eighteenth" has something for everyone, and very nice boulangeries too.

CHEZ WILLIAM

2, rue Francoeur

Métro line 12, Jules Joffrin Station

Autobus route 80

Telephone: 01-42-52-47-45

Open daily, except Monday, from 6:45 A.M. to 8:00 P.M.

When you visit the **Sacré-Coeur** and the **Place du Terte,** with its concentration of souvenir shops, be certain not to overlook the **Église St. Pierre,** one of the oldest churches in Paris, built in 1134. Boulangerie Chez William is a couple of blocks north. They bake several special breads, including a **pain rustique au seigle et fro-ment** (rye and wheat loaf) and **flûte à l'ancienne.** Fea-tured pastries include an attractive **puits d'amour** and a **brioche** with chocolate and custard. You will like their **gâteau au chocolat** (chocolate cake). Their quiches of several varieties, tarts, meringues, and macaroons are all notable. For those who don't speak French, don't worry; we were greeted by an English-speaking salesperson.

Le Cloërec, Jacques

111, rue Caulaincourt

Métro line 12, Lamarck Caulaincourt Station

Autobus route 80

Telephone: 01-46-06-75-08

Open daily from 7:45 A.M. to 8:00 P.M.

In the neighborhood of the **Sacré-Coeur** there are a number of interesting museums. **Musée Salvador Dali** and **Musée du Vieux Montmartre** are quite close to this delightful, small bakery north of the **Sacré-Coeur.** While the selection of bread is impressive, the pastries are what really catch your attention. Some are named after their street and neighborhood: **biscuit caulaincourt** and **pavé de montmartre.** Don't leave until you sample their **biscuit moëlleux chocolat avec glaçage à l'amande,** a mellow pastry with chocolate almond frosting. They also make their own chocolates and meringues. And English is spoken here.

$\mathscr{C}$OCHET

20, ave. de Clichy

Métro line 2 or 13, Place de Clichy Station

Autobus route 54, 74, 80, or 95

Telephone: 01-43-87-68-18

Open daily, except Sunday, from 7:30 A.M. to 8:00 P.M.

M. Cochet's authentic boulangerie has a complete selection of bread and many extras. Among his specialties we liked the **feuille d'amande et chocolat**, a layered almond and chocolate creation, and the **tartelettes aux fraises, framboises, kiwis, et bananes** (very small tarts topped with strawberries, raspberries, kiwi, and bananas). The display of **confitures** (jams) to complement the great breads is impressive. And they have fresh fruits, apples and pears, for sale.

$\mathscr{L}$ES $\mathscr{D}$ÉLICES DE $\mathscr{C}$USTINE

16, rue Custine

Métro line 4, Château Rouge Station

Autobus route 85

Telephone: 01-42-54-66-71

Open daily, except Thursday, from 6:30 A.M. to 9:00 P.M.

On rue Custine, where you begin the climb to the **Sacré-Coeur**, the unforgettable white church topping the **Montmartre** section of "the Eighteenth," we discovered this friendly corner bakery displaying the red Banette sign. They feature many of the breads made with this flour: **pain Banette levain, pain Banette fibre** (high-fiber bread), and **pain Banette complet.** The boulanger assured us these breads are made by the old-fashioned method. He is especially proud of his pastry creations and, if not busy, will take time to show you a book with pictures of his work for weddings and special occasions.

A U F EU DE B OIS

14, ave. de Clichy

Métro line 2 or 13, Place de Clichy Station

Autobus route 54, 74, 80, or 95

Telephone: 01-45-22-22-04

Open daily, except Sunday, from 6:30 A.M. to 8:30 P.M.

Just a short walk north of the busy Place de Clichy is M. Lagoutte's boulangerie, with an intriguing name that translates to "wood-fired," a sure sign of an authentic bakery. He features **pain de seigle** and chewy and tasty **pain aux céréales.** His pastries are also appealing, and we were attracted to small almond, pear, lemon, apricot, and even chocolate tarts. There are **croissants au jambon et fromage** (croissant sandwiches with ham and cheese) for takeout and several hot dishes—baked chicken, lasagna, and quiche.

GAMBINI

80, bis blvd. d'Ornano

Métro line 4, Porte de Clignancourt Station

Autobus route 56 or 85

Telephone: (none listed)

Open daily, except Wednesday, from 6:00 A.M. to 8:00 P.M.

At this bakery, you are just a short walk from **Les Puces**, the famous flea market, reputed to be Europe's largest, held Saturday, Sunday, and Monday from 7:00 A.M. to 7:30 P.M. Be prepared for crowds, since this attraction is on "the tourist route." At Les Puces, you will find clothing, antiques, leather, and many craft items from Africa and elsewhere. Boulangerie Gambini is a peaceful retreat, with a complete bread inventory and several sandwich innovations that are hard to turn down. Try their panini and croissants with a filling of ham and cheese.

GONTIER, SERGE

54, rue Custine

Métro line 12, Lamarck Caulaincourt Station, or Métro line 4,
     Château Rouge Station

Autobus route 85

Telephone: 01-42-64-33-81

Open daily, except Sunday, from 6:45 A.M. to 8:00 P.M.

M. Gontier's boulangerie is on the corner of rue Custine and rue Hermel, three blocks north of the **Basilique du**

Sacré-Coeur. You will enjoy the view of the city from the steps of the famous white church. It is particularly inspiring at dusk, as the vastness of Paris is defined by the lights. Stop by this small, neat shop on the way. They feature a **pain aux céréales** which was chewy and crusty in just the right proportions. Their flan, quiches, and sandwiches are also worth trying.

JEANNERET
69, blvd. Barbès
Métro line 4 or 12, Marcadet Poissonniers Station
Autobus route 31
Telephone: 01-46-06-18-26
Open daily, except Thursday, from 7:20 A.M. to 8:30 P.M.

On the busy boulevard Barbès, on the way up the hill to the **Porte de Clignancourt** and the famous flea market, we found a boulanger who specializes in bread and makes pastries as a sideline. Some of the bread defied translation to English, yet all are very enticing: **pain à fleur de coton, pain passion,** and the familiar **pain de seigle aux raisins** and **fougasse.** We have seen many other fougasses, but this one is a prize-winner.

Manzagol

33, ter rue Doudeauville

Métro line 4, Château Rouge Station

Autobus route 31, 65, or 80

Telephone: 01-46-06-13-11

Open daily, except Thursday, from 10:00 A.M. to 1:00 P.M. and
from 4:00 P.M. to 9:00 P.M.

As "bakery sleuths" we cannot play favorites, but if pressed to name a boulangerie we will not forget, it has to be Manzagol, a third-generation Paris boulangerie from a dynasty of boulangers originally from the Auvergne region. You will not find pastries, candy, or takeout foods here. They make only two kinds of bread—**pain au levain avec la farine de meule** and **pain de seigle**—stacked on an ancient wooden table visible from the street. The rye comes in two sizes and shapes, one weighing a bit less than 1 pound, the other over 4 pounds. The other bread is made from stone-ground flour. Take a step back in history to appreciate a genuine boulangerie.

MARGINIER

1, rue Custine
Métro line 4, Château Rouge Station
Telephone: 01-46-06-80-80
Open daily, except Tuesday, from 6:00 A.M. to 8:30 P.M.

You can't miss this bakery on the corner of rue Custine
and rue Poulet, with decorative glass panels on the outside of the store. This bakery is two blocks east of the
Sacré-Coeur, in a fascinating neighborhood of small
shops and cafés. M. Marginier has many bran, rye,
whole-wheat, and rustic loaves, and several sizes of
baguettes to tempt you: **pain de son, pain de seigle, pain
complet, pain bûcheron,** and **baguettes.** He also has a
small restaurant with a gourmet menu and takeout foods
and pastries, making this a choice stop in **Montmartre.**

MARY, JEAN-CLAUDE

50, rue Ordener
Métro line 4 or 12, Marcadet Poissonniers Station
Autobus route 31 or 60
Telephone: 01-46-06-46-83
Open daily, except Monday, from 8:00 A.M. to 2:00 P.M. and from
3:30 P.M. to 9:00 P.M.

Not far from the overpass that crosses the railroad tracks
north of the **Gare du Nord,** on rue Ordener, we located
this attractive corner boulangerie. This is the eastern

edge of "the Eighteenth," away from the tourist traffic of the Montmartre. You will enjoy the **pain en animaux** (bread in the shapes of animals), **pain au cumin,** and **ficelle viennoise,** a very thin Vienna loaf. The selection of takeout foods, especially the **quiche lorraine,** is tempting. You will also find a special cider from Normandie here.

Au Pain d'Antan

2, rue Eugène Sue

Métro line 4 or 12, Marcadet Poissonniers Station, or Métro line 12, Jules Joffrin Station

Autobus route 80 or 85

Telephone: 01-42-64-71-78

Open Monday from 7:00 A.M. to 1:00 P.M. and from 2:00 P.M. to 7:30 P.M.

Open Tuesday, Wednesday, and Thursday from 7:00 A.M. to 1:00 P.M. and from 4:00 P.M. to 7:30 P.M.

Open Friday from 7:00 A.M. to 7:00 P.M.

Open Saturday from 7:00 A.M. to 7:30 P.M.

Boulanger M. Sousa, from the Aveyron region, presides at this bakery with the reputation for some of the best sourdough bread in Paris. The name of this bakery means "bread from yesteryear," and his brick-lined oven dating from the early twenties continues to turn out prize-winning traditional **pain de campagne, pain de seigle, pain aux céréales,** and **pain de seigle aux noix et aux raisins.** No baguettes or flavored breads of any kind are baked here. They do bake a highly regarded specialty from the Aveyron region, **brioche** oozing in butter. It is said all of his grain breads will last one week. The **mairie** (town hall) for "the Eighteenth" is close by as you explore this north section of **Montmarte,** indeed one of the most enchanting sections of Paris.

𝒫ANORAMA, 𝒢UIS

62, blvd. Barbès

Métro line 4, Château Rouge Station, or Métro line 12, Marcadet
 Poissonniers Station

Telephone: 01-42-64-71-48

Open daily from 5:00 A.M. to 2:00 A.M.

This unusual boulangerie is a short walk north of the **Place du Château Rouge,** at the corner of blvd. Barbès and rue Doudeauville. It is staffed entirely by men, hard-working bakers and salesmen, who proudly advised us that we were in a Tunisian bakery with North African and French specialties. They feature traditional breads and others that were a bit difficult to identify but delightful to sample. Their selection of sweets, with cookies, glazed candies, and macaroons in abundance, is hard to pass up. We were treated to several samples with hot tea. These Tunisian bakers, in their bright, modern shop, will make a lasting impression on you, as they did on us.

La Petite Charlotte

24, rue des Abbesses

Métro line 12, Abbesses Station

Telephone: 01-46-06-18-77

Open daily, except Monday, from 7:00 A.M. to 8:00 P.M.

As you climb the hill west of the **Sacré-Coeur,** you will be rewarded if you stop at M. Blondeau's bakery, with its pink-and-blue front and sidewalk tables. Banette flour is used here in a full line of products, but there are some interesting variations, in particular a **pain aux noix et aux olives** (nut bread with olives) and **Banette fibre,** a high-fiber health loaf. The **croque-monsieur** is a popular choice to take to the outside tables. There are also tables inside and additional ones in a restaurant section next door, to accommodate the many visitors in **Montmartre.**

ARRONDISSEMENT

The story of "the Nineteenth" is one of renovation. We are told that Napoléon III, when exiled to England in his younger years, was impressed by the large public parks in London and that, when he became emperor of France, he determined that Paris too would have beautiful parks. He created four: Bois de Boulogne, Bois de Vincennes, Parc Montsouris and Parc des Buttes-Chaumont. The Parc des Buttes-Chaumont, in the southern part of "the Nineteenth," is an excellent example, and particularly interesting because of its history. The land it was built on was the site (from the thirteenth century until the Revolution) of the infamous gibbet, then the site of a garbage dump, next a breeding ground for fishing worms, and finally a gypsum quarry ("plaster of Paris"). Restoration and development of the park took 1,000 workers, toiling for four years. The soil was so badly contaminated that it had to be replaced before trees would grow. Caves, waterfalls, and a lake were all created to add interest to the park. Another attraction in "the Nineteenth" is La Villette, the ultra-modern city of science and industry, with hands-on shows and cultural entertainment. The Cité des Sciences et de l'Industrie was opened in 1985.

P. BOUTEAU

148, ave. Jean-Jaurès

Métro line 5, Ourcy Station

Telephone: 01-42-02-65-73

Open daily, except Sunday and Monday, from 6:00 A.M. to 8:00 P.M.

This small, friendly bakery is located an equal distance from **La Villette,** the **Canal de l'Ourcy,** and the **Parc des Buttes-Chaumont.** In addition to baguettes and boules, Bouteau features **pain complet biologique,** an organic bread with a distinctive taste. They offer a complete inventory of pastries, ranging from irresistible **truffes** (truffles) to **fouaces** (hearth cakes) and traditional pizza. Try their **forêt-noire,** a Black Forest cake with a special flair.

É. ET G. GUILLEBAUD

98, rue de Meaux

Métro line 5, Laumière Station

Telephone: 01-42-08-72-44

Open daily, except Sunday and Monday, from 7:00 A.M. to 8:30 P.M.

One of the largest parks in Paris, the **Parc des Buttes-Chaumont,** is only two blocks from the Laumière Metro station and M. Guillebaud's bakery; the park is a great place to enjoy your purchases from this fine shop. Try the country-style **campagrain** and the unique line of **pavé,** flat-baked cakes.

ORY, PASCAL

95, rue de Belleville

Métro line 11, Pyrénées Station

Autobus route 26

Telephone: 01-42-08-71-28

Open daily, except Sunday, from 6:45 A.M. to 8:15 P.M.

This bakery, located in a busy residential Belleville neighborhood, is open thirteen and a half hours per day. We sampled some of their outstanding bread—**pain des bois** and **pain boulanger**—and were tempted by their attractive croissants, their **gâteaux basques** (Basque cakes), **tarte au citron,** and **tarte normandie.** Their flan, petits fours, and meringues also caught our attention. **Parc de Belleville** is just a short walk away.

PAUL FARGES

26, rue Eugène Jumin

Métro line 5, Porte de Pantin Station

Autobus route 75

Telephone: 01-42-08-12-23

Open daily, except Monday and Tuesday, from 7:15 A.M. to 8:00 P.M.

Just a short walk from the **Conservatoire National de la Musique** and other attractions at **La Villette,** you will find Paul Farges's fascinating shop. The boulanger is especially proud of their special breads: **brioche, miche,** and **baguettes** of various lengths. Their **tartes alsaciennes** in several flavors—orange, apple, apricot—were impressive. They also make **truffes, flan,** and **gâteau au chocolat et Grand Marnier,** a very tempting cake, on the premises.

SARL SEPA

42, ave. Jean Jaurès

Métro line 5, Jaurès Station

Telephone: 01-42-00-10-50

Open daily, except Saturday and Sunday, from 7:00 A.M. to 8:00 P.M.

Close to Place de Stalingrad and the locks on the **Bassin de la Villette,** you will find this attractive boulangerie-pâtisserie. The baker features **pain à l'ancienne, pain polka,** and **pain au levain naturel.** In the pastry display they have **tartes aux pommes et au citron,** and they also have a choice of sandwiches for takeout.

J. ET F. SUZANNE

30, ave. de Laumière

Métro line 5, Laumière Station

Telephone: 01-42-08-49-67

Open Monday, Tuesday, Friday, Saturday, and Sunday from
7:00 A.M. to 9:00 P.M.

While these folks have an ample inventory of breads
baked on the premises, they list as their specialty
entremets au chocolat (chocolate sweets), also baked in
the shop. There are also cookies, large and small, and
tempting tarts and sandwiches. With the **Parc des
Buttes-Chaumont** a short walk away, the Suzanne
Boulangerie is a choice destination for lunch or snacks.

J. P. TANAY

116, rue de Meaux

Métro line 5, Laumière Station

Telephone: 01-42-08-70-45

Open daily, except Wednesday, from 7:00 A.M. to 8:00 P.M.

This is another bake shop with an extensive line of takeout delicacies—breads and pastries—that is well
located, a few short blocks from "the Nineteenth's" large
park the **Parc des Buttes-Chaumont.** We tried their
croissants au chocolat. They were worth the trip!

ARRONDISSEMENT

"The Twentieth" boasts a tumultuous past as the site of nineteenth-century political uprisings. "The Twentieth" was renowned as a workers' suburb in the nineteenth century, when Haussmann's ambitious rebuilding of the central city forced many to relocate to Belleville and Ménilmontant. Despite this, the arrondissement has retained its distinction as a working-class district. Its most famous and frequently visited attraction is the Cimetière du Père-Lachaise, developed and promoted by Napoléon in 1803. Over one million people are buried here (though there are only 100,000 grave markers), including French and foreign notables. Here lie the remains of Balzac, Rossini, Haussmann, Talleyrand, Molière, and a long list of other French luminaries as well as Chopin, Oscar Wilde, Gertrude Stein, and Jim Morrison, foreigners who were buried here because they died in Paris. The Père-Lachaise, immaculately landscaped with many trees and winding paths, must be one of the world's largest and best-known cemeteries. In "the Twentieth," a populous section of the city, you will find many bakeries.

ℬENINA

80, rue de Belleville

Métro line 11, Pyrénées Station

Autobus route 26

Telephone: 01-46-36-54-11

Open daily, except Wednesday, from 7:00 A.M. to 9:00 P.M.

Boulangerie Benina lists its specialties as French Oriental, and we noted several products giving the bakery this distinction. There are tarts and pies and a pizza-like pastry about six inches in diameter with anchovies. Their breads are most interesting and tend to have an Asian identity, quite different and worth trying.

ℬOULANGERIE DES ℘YRÉNÉES

304, rue des Pyrénées

Métro line 11, Jourdain Station

Autobus route 26

Telephone: 01-43-66-22-11

Open daily, except Wednesday, from 7:00 A.M. to 8:30 P.M.

Mme. Leconte operates this attractive bakery with a red-trimmed front in the north quarter of "the Twentieth."

There are several special breads, but **le païsou,** a hearty, odd-shaped country-style loaf, is a credit to the name of bread. They also have **croissants aux amandes, beignets** (doughnuts), and a line of sandwiches, some with **rillettes** (pork or goose liver spread). Children line up to select from the jars of penny candy and the fresh and chewy bread to eat on the way home from school.

 FOYART

> 143, blvd. Davout
>
> Métro line 3, Porte de Bagnolet Station
>
> Telephone: 01-48-81-20-38
>
> Open daily, except Saturday, from 6:30 A.M. to 8:30 P.M.

Foyart is on the extreme eastern edge of the city, and quite close to the several sports arenas in the vicinity of the **Porte de Bagnolet,** a major intersection on the highway around Paris. A large sign as you approach the bakery reads: "Pain cuit au bois" (bread baked in a wood-fired oven). This small corner bakery has a beamed ceiling, tile floors, and two interesting and attractive metal candelabra, and an impressive inventory of bread: **pain complet biologique, pain au levain** and **flûte bio 80%,** all organic leavened breads of quality. The pastry selection includes **flan, diplomates, tartelettes,** and more. It's well worth the trip!

𝒜ux 𝒢amins de 𝓜énilmontant

130, rue de Ménilmontant

Métro line 3, Gambetta Station

Autobus route 26 or 96

Telephone: 01-46-36-61-54

Open daily, except Wednesday, from 7:00 A.M. to 8:30 P.M.

This large corner bakery on the busy rue de Ménil-montant is a one-stop luncheon establishment, offering fresh-squeezed orange juice and wine with twenty vari-eties of bread, sandwiches, tarts, cookies, and mouth-watering pastries. They also display tempting **meringues à la vanille et au chocolat.**

𝓑. 𝒢anachaud (Jeudon, Père et Fils, successor to Monsieur Ganachaud)

150–152, rue de Ménilmontant

Métro line 3, Gambetta Station

Autobus route 26 or 96

Telephone: 01-46-36-13-82

Open Tuesday from 2:30 P.M. to 8:00 P.M.

Open Wednesday through Saturday from 7:30 A.M. to 8:00 P.M.

Open Sunday from 7:30 A.M. to 1:00 P.M.

Bernard Ganachaud, son of a master baker, was the first bread baker to win the prestigious Meilleur Ouvrier de France Award. The reputation for quality at this fine shop is secure, testified to by lines of hungry customers at all hours of the day. There are eight kneaded specialties and thirty breads of various shapes and weights, including their own creations: **le campagnard** and **la flûte gana.** A special pastry is featured each day, as are items on the extensive takeout shelves. We tried an open-faced **jambon et fromage** (ham and cheese sandwich) warmed to complete satisfaction. To top it off, they make their own ice cream and sorbet. Customers are able to watch as the boulanger working near the front of the shop kneads and shapes the dough—the boulanger can be seen from the interior of the shop or through a large window from the outside. It is well worth taking the time to stop here.

GÉRARD CHATEL

2, rue Ménilmontant

Métro line 2, Ménilmontant Station

Telephone: 01-46-36-95-65

Open daily from 6:30 A.M. to 8:00 P.M.

With the **Parc de Belleville** two blocks away, the Chatel bakery is well located for lunch in the park. A famous church, **Notre-Dame de la Croix,** is also close by. M. Chatel has an extensive line of takeouts in addition to all of the most popular breads.

HERBERT MARTIAL

75, ave. Gambetta

Métro line 3, Gambetta Station

Telephone: 01-46-36-60-59

Open daily, except Monday, from 6:00 A.M. to 8:00 P.M. and
Sunday mornings

M. Martial has twenty-three varieties of bread, every
shape and size to accommodate his steady stream of customers. He features several baguettes, some with poppy
seeds or sesame seeds and a **bag épis** decorated with a
stalk of wheat. The multigrain health breads are increas-
ingly popular. His are among the best. There are plenty
of takeouts here—sandwiches, quiches, pizzas, chocolates, and a variety of tarts.

HERVÉ TROIS

32, rue de Belleville

Métro line 11, Belleville Station or Pyrénées Station, or Métro line 2,
Belleville Station

Telephone: 01-46-36-59-51

Open daily, except Monday, from 6:30 A.M. to 8:00 P.M.

You can't miss this busy neighborhood bakery with
"Boulangerie" in large bold letters over its attractive window display. You will also note the authentic baker's sign
on the door, the familiar blue notice of bread baked on
the premises by an artisan baker—a sign visible in

almost all of the bakeries in this directory. In addition to a complete and irresistible selection of bread, Hervé Trois has some delectable pastries. They are especially proud of their **chaussons aux pommes** (apple turnovers), **tulipes** (tulip-shaped cookies), **financiers,** and chocolates. It is only a short walk from the **Parc de Belleville.**

Isabelle et Valerie

226, rue des Pyrénées
Metro line 3, Gambetta Station
Telephone: 01-43-58-42-62
Open daily, except Sunday and Monday, from 7:30 A.M. to
1:30 P.M. and from 2:30 P.M. to 8:00 P.M.

Carrying on the five-generation legacy as master bakers, Isabelle and Valerie Ganachaud, maîtres en boulangerie, daughters of Bernard Ganachaud, operate this busy corner bakery decorated with large terra cotta pots filled with plants, where customers form long lines for most of the day. They display many special breads. We were attracted to three in particular: **pain aux raisins et noisettes** (raisin and hazelnut bread), **campagne au germe de blé** (country-style loaf with wheat germ), and **pain organique.** This bakery is only a short distance from the **Cimetière du Père-Lachaise,** the main attraction in the arrondissement.

LE MOULE À GÂTEAU

243, rue des Pyrénées

Métro line 3, Gambetta Station

Telephone: 01-46-36-70-01

Open daily from 8:30 A.M. to 8:00 P.M.

This bakery has an interesting name, meaning "cake tin." While we found an abundant display of cakes, there was much more. The baker takes pride in his **pâtisseries artisanales,** pastries made without artificial coloring or preservatives and made with real butter. There were also many breads, and when we visited late in the afternoon, the shelves were nearly bare. We learned that this bakery produces baguettes, boules, and other breads several times each day, so you need not be at the shop when it opens to get that treasured loaf of hot bread. You only need to learn the hours when fresh, hot bread will be coming out of the oven.

PESCHEAUX

53, rue de Ménilmontant

Métro line 2, Ménilmontant Station

Autobus route 96

Telephone: 01-46-36-66-63

Open daily, except Tuesday, from 7:00 A.M. to 8:00 P.M.

In addition to a complete line of breads—baguettes baked in a circle and in various lengths as well as large, small, and multigrain boules—this neighborhood bakery bakes tempting pastries of many descriptions: **financiers, crème orange et citron** (orange and lemon custard), and a unique **noix de coco** (walnut-filled coconut). Pescheux is a short walk from the **Parc de Belleville,** "the Twentieth's" large park.

BIBLIOGRAPHY

Assire, Jerome. *The Book of Bread*. New York: Abbeville Press, 1996.

Brown, Edward Espe. *The Tassajara Bread Book*. Boston: Shambhala, 1995.

Chelminski, Rudolph. "Any Way You Slice It a Poilâne Loaf Is REAL French Bread." *Smithsonian* (January 1995).

Child, Julia. *Mastering the Art of French Cooking*, volumes I and II. New York: Alfred A. Knopf, 1970.

Clayton, Bernard, Jr. *Complete Book of Small Breads*. New York: Simon & Schuster, 1998.

——. *New Complete Book of Breads*. New York: Simon & Schuster, 1987.

——. *The Breads of France*. Indianapolis, Ind.: Macmillan, 1978.

Dannenberg, Linda. *Paris Boulangerie-Pâtisserie*. New York: Clarkson/Potter, 1994.

Desmons, Giles. *Walking Paris*. Lincolnwood, Ind.: Passport Books, 1997.

Donovan, Maria, et al. contribs. *France: A Culinary Journey*. Chino Hills, Calif.: Collins Publishers, 1992.

Fitch, Noel Riley. *Walks in Hemingway's Paris*. New York: St. Martin's Press, 1990.

"France's Daily Bread to Be Regulated." *Tulsa World,* January 4, 1997.

Gayot, André, Sheila Mooney, and Stephanie Masson, eds. *The Best of Paris, Île de France, and the Loire Valley*. Los Angeles: Gayot Publications, 1997.

Harrison, John. *The Cuisine of Hubert Keller*. Berkeley, Calif: Ten Speed Press, 1996.

Leader, Daniel, and Judith Blahnik. *Bread Alone*. New York: William Morrow, 1993.

Middleditch, Michael. *The Paris Mapguide*. New York: Viking Penguin, 1994.

Ortiz, Joe. *The Village Baker*. Berkeley, Calif.: Ten Speed Press, 1993.

Paris Plan. Tours, France: Michelin Travel Publications, 1996.

Simpson, Carole, and Jim Wooten. ABC News Transcript #701, "A Loaf of Bread, a Jug of Wine, and Thou...: French government regulations re: Boulangeries." World News Sunday, January 5, 1997.

Time-Life Recipes: Classic French Cooking. Alexandria, Va.: Time-Life Books, 1970.

Wells, Patricia. *Patricia Wells at Home in Provence.* New York: Scribner, 1996.

——. *The Food Lover's Guide to Paris.* New York: Workman, 1993.

——. *The Food Lover's Guide to France.* New York: Workman, 1987.

Wurman, Richard Saul. *Access Paris.* New York: Harper-Collins, 1998.

INDEX

Jack Armstrong was born in Philadelphia and grew up in South Bend, Indiana. A graduate of DePauw University with a major in European history, he first saw Paris from the back of an army truck in 1945 and has since returned ten times, always fascinated by its history and culinary supremacy, and especially its boulangeries. Jack's career has been as a professional Boy Scout executive with assignments in Missouri, Iowa, Colorado, and New Jersey. He was president of American Humanics, a national educational foundation, for seven years and served as an adjunct faculty member at Arizona State University for three years. He resides in Arizona and Missouri.

Delores Wilson is a native of Tulsa, Oklahoma, and attended St. Mary's College, where she majored in journalism, studying also at the University of Chicago and the University of Missouri. Her career has been in higher education as an administrative assistant to the president of American Humanics and the chancellor emeritus of the University of Missouri. Currently, she is a corporate travel consultant in Shawnee, Kansas, where she makes her home.